Introduction

Thank you for choosing this book. I hope you find the questions challenging, entertaining and interesting.

These questions come from a year's worth of news as I write a weekly current affairs quiz called 'The Dozen' which is published on my site www.ralphsquiz.com

As you recall the answers, I trust they will take you through the tales of the year 2023. It has been interesting to see them again, in the context of an annual compilation looking back over 12 months instead of the immediacy of their initial week to week usage. I have a pretty good memory but I found some of these questions challenging with the passing of time, albeit short term - and I wrote them!

Inside you will find over 500 questions, right up to and including December 2023, so this really is a Big Quiz of the Year.

If you are a quiz master, this is sure to help out as you prepare for the festive season and if you are not, it is still sure to provide you, your family and friends with some great entertainment as you celebrate the holidays.

One final note: Up to December, there are at least 40 questions for every month, but the number of questions vary and I know this irritates some people. I wasn't going to leave a question out just because of working to a set value, so I'm afraid if it irritates, it will have to. I'm sure that there is plenty there for you to be selective with and I would rather leave you with that choice.

I sincerely hope you enjoy the questions.

Michael Baker December 2023

THE BIG QUIZ OF 2023

Michael Baker

Copyright © 2023 Michael Baker

All rights reserved

No part of this book may be reproduced, or stored in a retrieval system, or transmitted in any form or by any means, electronic, mechanical, photocopying, recording, or otherwise, without express written permission of the publisher.

Cover design by: Michael Baker

ISBN: 9798870673653

THE BIG QUIZ OF 2023

Table of Contents

Introduction 1
January 2023 - Questions 5
January 2023 – Answers 9
February 2023 - Questions 13
February 2023 - Answers 16
March 2023 - Questions 19
March 2023 - Answers 23
April 2023 - Questions 27
April 2023 - Answers 31
May 2023 - Questions 35
May 2023 - Answers 39
June 2023 - Questions 44
June 2023 - Answers 48
July 2023 - Questions 52
July 2023 - Answers 56
August 2023 - Questions 60
August 2023 - Answer 64
September 2023 - Questions 69
September 2023 - Answers 73
October 2023 - Questions 77
October 2023 - Answers 81
November 2023 - Questions 85
November 2023 - Answers 89
December 2023 - Questions 94
December 2023 - Answers 97
Books By This Author 100
Thank You 101

January 2023 - Questions

1. Queen guitarist Brian May was given a knighthood in the New Years Honours list, but what has he traditionally used as a plectrum?
2. Thor, the walrus was back in the news, which council sagely called off their New Years firework display so as not to cause him stress?
3. Who became the PDC World Champion Darts Player for 2023?
4. It was reported that Rishi Sunak wanted all students to study which subject until age 18?
5. Cristiano Ronaldo joined a football club in which country?
6. In The Masked Singer, *Ghost* became the first to leave the 2023 competition. Who was behind the mask?
7. Sadly, Pele arguably the worlds greatest ever footballer passed away. He visited England in 1972 and 1973 where he played in friendlies for his club side against clubs including Aston Villa, Plymouth Argyle and Sheffield Wednesday. What was his club side called?
8. It was announced that from January 5th, travellers from which country would need to provide a negative COVID test before boarding a plane to England?
9. Which UK tv channel aired an interview with Prince Harry as he sought publicity for his new book?
10. And which journalist interviewed Prince Harry for the programme?
11. Which former Pope sadly passed away aged 95?
12. Which school based soap relocated again, this time from Scotland to return to tv screens in January?

13. Which then League 2 side knocked Aston Villa out of the FA Cup?
14. Which country saw riots at government buildings following the recent swearing in of their new President?
15. Rishi Sunak was criticised for taking an internal flight to visit which British city?
16. Which county was the base for the Spaceport from which the Virgin Orbit mission took off?
17. Patsy Palmer and John Fashanu were announced in the line up of competitors for which TV competition?
18. A consignment of scrap metal containing Uranium was reportedly detected at which airport?
19. *The Fabelmans* won a best director at the Golden Globe Awards for who?
20. In US politics, who was finally elected as Speaker for the House of Representatives after 15 rounds?
21. Who's single *Made You Look* returned to the Top 5 in the UK Singles Chart?
22. Which legendary presenter announced they would be leaving BBC Radio 2?
23. Who scored Manchester United's controversial equalising goal in the derby with Manchester City?
24. Who was behind the mask as *Piece of Cake* in the latest edition of The Masked Singer?
25. What is the brand name of the hydration drink marketed by YouTubers KSI ad Logan Paul?
26. The Harbin Ice Show boasted 2,000 displays. In which country is it held?
27. Which daytime show had Colin Murray declared as its new permanent host?

28. Greta Thunberg posted that she was part of a group detained briefly for protesting an open cast coal mine in which country?
29. Which couple, well known for winning Strictly Come Dancing, announced the birth of their baby daughter?
30. Which legendary performer announced their upcoming Celebration Tour marking over 40 years as a recording artist?
31. Which NFL team were eliminated from the playoffs, sparking speculation about whether quarterback Tom Brady might retire?
32. Which Prime Minister announced their resignation citing burnout?
33. A tale of 2 Astronauts: Firstly, which British astronaut announced his retirement and secondly, which astronaut married for the 4th time aged 93?
34. The next Lunar New Year was celebrated. Which animal is associated with it?
35. Which Scottish Premier League team were knocked out of the Scottish Cup by non-league Darvel?
36. How many Oscar nominations did *Everything Everywhere All At Once* receive?
37. Who was the current German Chancellor?
38. Comet C/2022 E3 (ZTF) neared its closest distance from the Earth. What colour in its appearance makes it special?
39. In Scotland, their biggest union is the EIS, in England and Wales it is the NEU. Which profession do they represent?
40. Who was sacked as manager of Everton FC?
41. What motoring offence warranted a fine for Prime Minister Rishi Sunak?
42. The slogan 'United By Music' was revealed in the official handover of what to Liverpool at the end of the month?

43. Which golfer won the Dubai Desert Classic?

44. Which (now) annual charity event revealed a significant overhaul to its iconic item of wear? - One change being that it is now manufactured from 95% plant based material rather than plastic?

45. The Royal Mint unveiled a new design for a collectors coin. As well as King Charles III, the reverse features which Tudor monarch?

46. Which Rock legend announced his retirement from touring, due to the physical demand, at the age of 74, cancelling his Europe and UK farewell shows?

47. Chelsea broke the British transfer record on the last day of the January transfer window, signing Enzo Fernandez from which club?

48. Who was sacked by Rishi Sunak as Tory Party Chair?

49. Which tennis player won the Australian Open Womens Singles title?

50. Who remained in top spot on the UK Singles Chart with *Flowers*?

January 2023 – Answers

1. Queen guitarist Brian May was given a knighthood in the New Years Honours list, but what has he traditionally used as a plectrum? **A sixpence**

2. Thor, the walrus was back in the news, which council sagely called off their New Years firework display so as not to cause him stress? **Scarborough**

3. Who became the PDC World Champion Darts Player for 2023? **Michael Smith**

4. It was reported that Rishi Sunak wanted all students to study which subject until age 18? **Maths**

5. Cristiano Ronaldo joined a football club in which country? **Saudi Arabia**

6. In The Masked Singer, *Ghost* became the first to leave the 2023 competition. Who was behind the mask? **Chris Kamara**

7. Sadly, Pele arguably the worlds greatest ever footballer passed away. He visited England in 1972 and 1973 where he played in friendlies for his club side against clubs including Aston Villa, Plymouth Argyle and Sheffield Wednesday. What was his club side called? **Santos**

8. It was announced that from January 5th, travellers from which country would need to provide a negative COVID test before boarding a plane to England? **China**

9. Which UK tv channel aired an interview with Prince Harry as he sought publicity for his new book? **ITV1 or ITVx**

10. And which journalist interviewed Prince Harry for the programme? **Tom Bradby**

11. Which former Pope sadly passed away aged 95? **Pope Benedict XVI**

12. Which school based soap relocated again, this time from Scotland to return to tv screens in January? **Waterloo Road**

13. Which then League 2 side knocked Aston Villa out of the FA Cup? **Stevenage**

14. Which country saw riots at government buildings following the recent swearing in of their new President? **Brazil**

15. Rishi Sunak was criticised for taking an internal flight to visit which British city? **Leeds**

16. Which county was the base for the Spaceport from which the Virgin Orbit mission took off? **Cornwall**

17. Patsy Palmer and John Fashanu were announced in the line up of competitors for which TV competition? **Dancing on Ice**

18. A consignment of scrap metal containing Uranium was reportedly detected at which airport? **Heathrow**

19. *The Fabelmans* won a best director at the Golden Globe Awards for who? **Steven Spielberg**

20. In US politics, who was finally elected as Speaker for the House of Representatives after 15 rounds? **Kevin McCarthy**

21. Who's single *Made You Look* returned to the Top 5 in the UK Singles Chart? **Meghan Trainor**

22. Which legendary presenter announced they would be leaving BBC Radio 2? **Ken Bruce**

23. Who scored Manchester United's controversial equalising goal in the derby with Manchester City? **Bruno Fernandes**

24. Who was behind the mask as *Piece of Cake* in the latest edition of The Masked Singer? **Lulu**

25. What is the brand name of the hydration drink marketed by YouTubers KSI ad Logan Paul? **Prime**

26. The Harbin Ice Show boasted 2,000 displays. In which country is it held? **China**

27. Which daytime show had Colin Murray declared as its new permanent host? **Countdown**

28. Greta Thunberg posted that she was part of a group detained briefly for protesting an open cast coal mine in which country? **Germany**

29. Which couple, well known for winning Strictly Come Dancing, announced the birth of their baby daughter? **Stacey Dooley and Kevin Clifton**

30. Which legendary performer announced their upcoming Celebration Tour marking over 40 years as a recording artist? **Madonna**

31. Which NFL team were eliminated from the playoffs, sparking speculation about whether quarterback Tom Brady might retire? **Tampa Bay Buccaneers**

32. Which Prime Minister announced their resignation citing burnout? **Jacinda Ardern**

33. A tale of 2 Astronauts: Firstly, which British astronaut announced his retirement and secondly, which astronaut married for the 4th time aged 93? **Tim Peake and Buzz Aldrin**

34. The next Lunar New Year was celebrated. Which animal is associated with it? **Rabbit**

35. Which Scottish Premier League team were knocked out of the Scottish Cup by non-league Darvel? **Aberdeen**

36. How many Oscar nominations did *Everything Everywhere All At Once* receive? **Eleven**

37. Who is the current German Chancellor? **Olaf Scholz**

38. Comet C/2022 E3 (ZTF) neared its closest distance from the Earth. What colour in its appearance makes it special? **Green**

39. In Scotland, their biggest union is the EIS, in England and Wales it is the NEU. Which profession do they represent? **Teachers**

40. Who was sacked as manager of Everton FC? **Frank Lampard**

41. What motoring offence warranted a fine for Prime Minister Rishi Sunak? **Not wearing a seatbelt**

42. The slogan 'United By Music' was revealed in the official handover of what to Liverpool at the end of the month? **The Eurovision Song Contest**

43. Which golfer won the Dubai Desert Classic? **Rory McIlroy**

44. Which (now) annual charity event revealed a significant overhaul to its iconic item of wear? - One change being that it is now manufactured from 95% plant based material rather than plastic. **Red Nose Day**

45. The Royal Mint unveiled a new design for a collectors coin. As well as King Charles III, the reverse features which Tudor monarch? **Henry VIII**

46. Which Rock legend announced his retirement from touring, due to the physical demand, at the age of 74, cancelling his Europe and UK farewell shows? **Ozzy Osbourne**

47. Chelsea broke the British transfer record on the last day of the January transfer window, signing Enzo Fernandez from which club? **Benfica**

48. Who was sacked by Rishi Sunak as Tory Party Chair? **Nadhim Zahawi**

49. Which tennis player won the Australian Open Womens Singles title? **Aryna Sabalenka**

50. Who remained in top spot on the UK Singles Chart with *Flowers*? **Miley Cyrus**

February 2023 - Questions

1. Who won the NFL Super Bowl?
2. It was announced that Queen Consort Camilla's crown would not contain which controversial diamond?
3. Which town in Kent was the location of a new Banksy artwork called Valentine's Day Mascara?
4. Who won the *Best New Act* award at the Brit Awards?
5. In the Men's Six Nations, who scored 2 tries for Scotland as they beat Wales 35-7?
6. Which fizzy drink, first launched in 1975 was renamed *Fanta Pineapple and Grapefruit* from Valentine's Day onwards?
7. Which politician announced her resignation on 15th February?
8. Which legendary songwriter who's works included *Alfie, I Say a Little Prayer* and *This Guy's in Love With You* passed away, sadly, aged 94?
9. Who's song *Red Flags* claimed top spot in the UK Singles Chart?
10. Which F1 team reverted back to a black livery following the silver they raced in last season?
11. In a contest held in February, John Lydon's PIL missed out on the opportunity to represent which country at Eurovision this year?
12. The US Military shot down a suspect spy balloon. This was over the coast of which state?
13. Who won the Calcutta Cup?
14. The final episode of Happy Valley was broadcast. What is the name of Sarah Lancashire's character?

15. Brad Hall, Taylor Lawrence, Greg Cackett and Arran Gulliver won a silver medal at the IBSF World Championships in what event?
16. The UK government underwent a cabinet reshuffle. Who was appointed to the Tory Party Chairman post?
17. Who won the Grammy for *Album of the Year 2023*?
18. Which Premier League football club were charged with breaking its financial rules?
19. Who became the NBA's all-time leading scorer, passing Kareem Abdul-Jabbar's 39-year-old record of 38,387 points?
20. The Commonwealth Games Bull finally found a permanent home in Birmingham. Whereabouts?
21. In a departure from his usual vocation, who released a sauce brand range called Tingly Ted's?
22. Which football manager became the subject of a new National Theatre play?
23. Ricky Wilson from The Kaiser Chiefs was runner up in this years Masked Singer TV competition. Which character/costume did he wear?
24. England beat New Zealand in the First Test Match of their series. How many wickets in total did James Anderson and Stuart Broad take in New Zealand's second innings?
25. In the Southern Hemisphere, which February event takes place in the Sambadrome?
26. Which authors books were in the news this week due to them being controversially airbrushed in a review conducted by the publishers?
27. And which popular publishing house declared they were releasing a Childrens book about Climate Change which has been co-authored by King Charles?
28. Which movie won the Best Film Award at the BAFTA's?

29. A conservation project planned to reintroduce wildcats to which part of Britain? A: Snowdonia B: Devon and Cornwall C: The North of Scotland D: Northumbria

30. Which TV Soap featured a flash forward to Christmas 2023?

31. What sort of animal, nicknamed Godzilla was found away from its normal habitat in a New York park?

32. Which artists album *Queen of Me* reached top spot on the UK Charts?

33. The final commemorative stamps to bear the Queen's head were revealed. What was their subject?

34. Who won the Carabao Cup Final?

35. Which atmospheric phenomenon was visible in Britain as far South as Cornwall?

36. The first woman to become Speaker of the House of Commons passed away, sadly, this month. What is her name?

37. Mia Brookes became the youngest World Champion to date in what sport?

38. Who is the European Commission President who had meetings with Rishi Sunak and also King Charles?

39. A feature length movie about DCI John Luther appeared on cinema screens. Who plays the title role in *Luther: Falling Sun*?

40. Pink's new album went straight to Number One spot on the UK album chart. What is its title?

February 2023 - Answers

1. Who won the NFL Super Bowl? **Kansas City Chiefs**
2. It was announced that Queen Consort Camilla's crown would not contain which controversial diamond? **koh-I-noor**
3. Which town in Kent was the location of a new Banksy artwork called Valentine's Day Mascara? **Margate**
4. Who won the *Best New Act* award at the Brit Awards? **Wet Leg**
5. In the Men's Six Nations, who scored 2 tries for Scotland as they beat Wales 35-7? **Kyle Steyn**
6. Which fizzy drink, first launched in 1975 was renamed *Fanta Pineapple and Grapefruit* from Valentine's Day onwards? **Lilt**
7. Which politician announced her resignation on 15th February? **Nicola Sturgeon**
8. Which legendary songwriter who's works included *Alfie, I Say a Little Prayer* and *This Guy's in Love With You* passed away, sadly, aged 94? **Burt Bacharach**
9. Who's song *Red Flags* claimed top spot in the UK Singles Chart? **Mimi Webb**
10. Which F1 team reverted back to a black livery following the silver they raced in last season? **Mercedes**
11. In a contest held in February, John Lydon's PIL missed out on the opportunity to represent which country at Eurovision this year? **Ireland**
12. The US Military shot down a suspect spy balloon. This was over the coast of which state? **South Carolina**
13. Who won the Calcutta Cup? **Scotland**

14. The final episode of Happy Valley was broadcast. What is the name of Sarah Lancashire's character? **Catherine Cawood**

15. Brad Hall, Taylor Lawrence, Greg Cackett and Arran Gulliver won a silver medal at the IBSF World Championships in what event? **4 Man Bobsleigh**

16. The UK government underwent a cabinet reshuffle. Who was appointed to the Tory Party Chairman post? **Greg Hands**

17. Who won the Grammy for *Album of the Year 2023*? **Harry Styles**

18. Which Premier League football club were charged with breaking its financial rules? **Manchester City**

19. Who became the NBA's all-time leading scorer, passing Kareem Abdul-Jabbar's 39-year-old record of 38,387 points? **LeBron James**

20. The Commonwealth Games Bull finally found a permanent home in Birmingham. Whereabouts? **New Street Station**

21. In a departure from their usual vocation, who released a sauce brand range called Tingly Ted's? **Ed Sheeran**

22. Which football manager became the subject of a new National Theatre play? **Gareth Southgate**

23. Ricky Wilson from The Kaiser Chiefs was runner up in this years Masked Singer TV competition. Which character/costume did he wear? **Phoenix**

24. England beat New Zealand in the First Test Match of their series. How many wickets in total did James Anderson and Stuart Broad take in New Zealand's second innings? **Eight (4 each)**

25. In the Southern Hemisphere, which February event takes place in the Sambadrome? **Rio Carnival**

26. Which authors books were in the news this week due to them being controversially airbrushed in a review conducted by the publishers? **Roald Dahl**

27. And which popular publishing house declared they were releasing a Childrens book about Climate Change which has been co-authored by King Charles? **Ladybird**

28. Which movie won the Best Film Award at the BAFTA's? **All Quiet on the Western Front**

29. A conservation project planned to reintroduce wildcats to which part of Britain? A: Snowdonia B: Devon and Cornwall C: The North of Scotland D: Northumbria **B**

30. Which TV Soap featured a flash forward to Christmas 2023? **Eastenders**

31. What sort of animal, nicknamed Godzilla was found away from its normal habitat in a New York park? **Alligator**

32. Which artists album *Queen of Me* reached top spot on the UK Charts? **Shania Twain**

33. The final stamps to bear the Queen's head were revealed. What was their subject? **100 years of the Flying Scotsman**

34. Who won the Carabao Cup Final? **Manchester United**

35. Which atmospheric phenomenon was visible in Britain as far South as Cornwall? **Aurora Borealis**

36. The first woman to become Speaker of the House of Commons passed away, sadly, this month. What is her name? **Betty Boothroyd**

37. Mia Brookes became the youngest World Champion to date in what sport? **Snowboarding**

38. Who is the European Commission President who met with Rishi Sunak and also King Charles? **Ursula Von der Leyen**

39. A feature length movie about DCI John Luther appeared on cinema screens. Who plays the title role in *Luther: Falling Sun*? **Idris Elba**

40. Pink's new album went straight to Number One spot on the UK album chart. What is its title? **Trustful**

March 2023 - Questions

1. Which UK nation celebrates its Patron Saints Day on March 1st?
2. What new role at the BBC was undertaken by Vernon Kay this month?
3. Which Championship football team appointed their third manager of the season after Chris Wilder took over?
4. Mattel announced that they intend to release a Barbie Role Model Doll of Dr Maggie Aderin-Pocock. With what field of Science is she associated?
5. Guns N' Roses and Arctic Monkeys were the latest headline acts to be announced to appear at which Festival? A: Glastonbury, B: Reading and Leeds, C: Isle of Wight or D: Party in the Park
6. Which Ferrari driver failed to complete the race distance in the opening F1 GP in Bahrain?
7. Which newspaper received Matt Hancock's WhatsApp messages when they were passed on by Isabel Oakeshott?
8. Which event sold out of its tickets in less than an hour when they went on sale at 12 Noon Tuesday 7th March?
9. Which religion celebrates the festival of Holi?
10. What is the name of the new music quiz segment on Radio 2's mid-morning show?
11. Which League 2 side reached the quarter-finals of the FA Cup?
12. Abby Cook became the 42nd presenter of which TV programme?
13. Jeff Reitz from California set a world record by visiting Disneyland Resort Los Angeles daily for how many days straight? A: 29 B: 731 C: 1,058 or D: 2,995

14. Although they lost their last One Day International, England's cricketers won the series 2-1. Who did they beat?

15. Who is the Director General of the BBC?

16. Which bank bought the UK arm of the Silicon Valley Bank after its Californian parent company reportedly collapsed?

17. England's rugby team suffered a big defeat in the Six Nations to France. How many points did France score at Twickenham?

18. How many Oscars did Everything, Everywhere All at Once win?

19. The Cheltenham Festival got underway in its usual March slot. Which county is Cheltenham in?

20. A set of special stamps on the theme of garden flowers will be the first to feature the silhouette of King Charles. In all there are ten stamps each featuring a type of flower. How many can you name?

21. Why was a Lagotto Romagnolo in the news this month?

22. With international football starting up again for the calendar year, who was reportedly set to replace Gareth Bale as captain of Wales?

23. Who bestowed the knighthood on Brian May in a ceremony this month?

24. Brian May's wife accompanied him to Buckingham Palace. What is her name?

25. Sadly, Dick Fosbury, the athlete who developed the *Fosbury Flop* high jump technique passed away. At which Olympics did he win the gold medal?

26. Budget Day arrived in March, which Chancellor of the Exchequer delivered their speech?

27. Which institution was the subject of a report called *The Casey Review*?

28. It was announced that at the age of 92, Rupert Murdoch was set to marry again. How many times would this be?
29. Which Championship team won through to the semi-finals of the Emirates FA Cup?
30. Which 2 contestants reached the final of this year's *The Apprentice* (UK)? (First Names only)
31. Which horse won The Cheltenham Gold Cup?
32. BBC's *Morning Live* presenter, Gethin Jones danced for 24 hours to raise money for which charity?
33. What was Boris Johnson's constituency?
34. Who won the F1 Saudi Arabian Grand Prix?
35. In the Rugby Six Nations, which team completed the Grand Slam with victory over England?
36. The Lead Singer of the Cure said he was *'sickened'* by Ticketmaster fees. What is his name?
37. What is the name of Google's potential chatbot rival to ChatGPT?
38. Who is the new First Minister of Scotland?
39. Which company owned the 3 firms fined over 19 million pounds by the Gambling Comission for reportedly failing to protect consumers and weak anti-money laundering controls?
40. Which is the longer distance; the Boat Race course or the Grand National course?
41. According to the Sunday Times, Wadhurst is the best place to live in the UK. In which county is it?
42. Which footballer became England Mens leading goalscorer of all time following a victory over Italy?
43. Which 5 planets were visible in a straight line, known as a *Planetary Parade* on Tuesday?

44. Where in Dorset was the subject of a spill of liquid containing oil, leading to concern for the environment?

45. Selina Gomez was reported to have become the most followed woman on Instagram. How many followers has she accumulated to date? A: 4 million B: 40 million C: 400 million or D: 4,000 million

46. Which sportswoman, who held the world record for the most caps of any female rugby player, decided to retire from the sport and played their last match in a Six Nations game against Scotland?

47. *Songs of Surrender* is the title of a Number One album in the UK charts. Which legendary group recorded it?

48. King Charles' first scheduled state visit to a European country was postponed. Which country was he due to travel to?

49. Which Motorway connects the M25 London Orbital with the port of Dover?

50. Why were Christina Koch, Victor Glover, Reid Wiseman and Jeremy Hansen in the news at the end of the month?

March 2023 - Answers

1. Which UK nation celebrates its Patron Saints Day on March 1st? **Wales**

2. What new role at the BBC was undertaken by Vernon Kay this month? **Host of the mid-morning show on Radio 2**

3. Which Championship football team appointed their third manager of the season after Chris Wilder took over? **Watford**

4. Mattel announced that they intend to release a Barbie Role Model Doll of Dr Maggie Aderin-Pocock. With what field of Science is she associated? **Astronomy**

5. Guns N' Roses and Arctic Monkeys were the latest headline acts to be announced to appear at which Festival? A: Glastonbury, B: Reading and Leeds, C: Isle of Wight or D: Party in the Park **A**

6. Which Ferrari driver failed to complete the race distance in the opening F1 GP in Bahrain? **Charles LeClerc**

7. Which newspaper received Matt Hancock's WhatsApp messages when they were passed on by Isabel Oakeshott? **The Daily Telegraph**

8. Which event sold out of its tickets in less than an hour when they went on sale at 12 Noon Tuesday 7th March? **Eurovision 2023**

9. Which religion celebrates the festival of Holi? **Hindu**

10. What is the name of the new music quiz segment on Radio 2's mid-morning show? **Ten to the top**

11. Which League 2 side reached the quarter-finals of the FA Cup? **Grimsby Town**

12. Abby Cook became the 42nd presenter of which TV programme? **Blue Peter**

13. Jeff Reitz from California set a world record by visiting Disneyland Resort Los Angeles daily for how many days straight? A: 29 B: 731 C: 1,058 or D: 2,995 **D**

14. Although they lost their last One Day International, England's cricketers won the series 2-1. Who did they beat? **Bangladesh**

15. Who is the Director General of the BBC? **Tim Davie**

16. Which bank bought the UK arm of the Silicon Valley Bank after its Californian parent company reportedly collapsed? **HSBC**

17. England's rugby team suffered a big defeat in the Six Nations to France. How many points did France score at Twickenham? **53**

18. How many Oscars did Everything, Everywhere All at Once win? **7**

19. The Cheltenham Festival got underway in its usual March slot. Which county is Cheltenham in? **Gloucestershire**

20. A set of special stamps on the theme of garden flowers will be the first to feature the silhouette of King Charles. In all there are ten stamps each featuring a type of flower. How many can you name? **Sweet Pea, Lily, Iris, Sunflower, Fuschia, Tulip, Peony, Nasturtium, Rose and Dahlia**

21. Why was a Lagotto Romagnolo in the news this month? **It was the first time this breed had won 'Best in Show' at Crufts**

22. With international football starting up again for the calendar year, who was reportedly set to replace Gareth Bale as captain of Wales? **Aaron Ramsay**

23. Who bestowed the knighthood on Brian May in a ceremony this month? **King Charles**

24. Brian May's wife accompanied him to Buckingham Palace. What is her name? **Anita Dobson**

25. Sadly, Dick Fosbury, the athlete who developed the *Fosbury Flop* high jump technique passed away. At which Olympics did he win the gold medal? **Mexico 1968**

26. Budget Day arrived in March, which Chancellor of the Exchequer delivered their speech? **Jeremy Hunt**

27. Which institution was the subject of a report called *The Casey Review*? **The Met Police**

28. It was announced that at the age of 92, Rupert Murdoch was set to marry again. How many times would this be? **5**

29. Which Championship team won through to the semi-finals of the Emirates FA Cup? **Sheffield United**

30. Which 2 contestants reached the final of this year's *The Apprentice* (UK)? (First Names only) **Rochelle and Marnie**

31. Which horse won The Cheltenham Gold Cup? **Galopin des Champs**

32. BBC's *Morning Live* presenter, Gethin Jones danced for 24 hours to raise money for which charity? **Comic Relief**

33. What was Boris Johnson's constituency? **Uxbridge and South Ruislip**

34. Who won the F1 Saudi Arabian Grand Prix? **Sergio Perez#**

35. In the Rugby Six Nations, which team completed the Grand Slam with victory over England? **Ireland**

36. The Lead Singer of the Cure said he was *'sickened'* by Ticketmaster fees. What is his name? **Robert Smith**

37. What is the name of Google's potential chatbot rival to ChatGPT? **Bard**

38. Who is the new First Minister of Scotland? **Humza Yousaf**

39. Which company owned the 3 firms fined over 19 million pounds by the Gambling Comission for reportedly failing to protect consumers and weak anti-money laundering controls? **William Hill**

40. Which is the longer distance; the Boat Race course or the Grand National course? **The Grand National Course**

41. According to the Sunday Times, Wadhurst is the best place to live in the UK. In which county is it? **East Sussex**

42. Which footballer became England Mens leading goalscorer of all time following a victory over Italy? **Harry Kane**

43. Which 5 planets were visible in a straight line, known as a *Planetary Parade* on Tuesday? **Jupiter, Mercury, Venus, Uranus and Mars**

44. Where in Dorset was the subject of a spill of liquid containing oil, leading to concern for the environment? **Poole Harbour**

45. Selina Gomez was reported to have become the most followed woman on Instagram. How many followers has she accumulated to date? A: 4 million B: 40 million C: 400 million or D: 4,000 million **C**

46. Which sportswoman, who held the world record for the most caps of any female rugby player, decided to retire from the sport and played their last match in a Six Nations game against Scotland? **Sarah Hunter**

47. *Songs of Surrender* is the title of a Number One album in the UK charts. Which legendary group recorded it? **U2**

48. King Charles' first scheduled state visit to a European country was postponed. Which country was he due to travel to? **France**

49. Which Motorway connects the M25 London Orbital with the port of Dover? **M20**

50. Why were Christina Koch, Victor Glover, Reid Wiseman and Jeremy Hansen in the news at the end of the month? **They were named as the crew for the Artemis 2 Moon mission**

April 2023 - Questions

1. After Antonio Conté left Tottenham Hotspur, which two Premier League football clubs sacked their managers/head coaches at the start of April?

2. Sadly, Paul O'Grady passed away. What was the name of his Television and Stage drag persona?

3. Which European country was the subject of King Charles First State visit?

4. An investigation conducted by the Information Commissioner's Office (ICO) found which popular video sharing app breached data protection law and fined it £12.7 million?

5. *Standing at the Sky's Edge* won 'Best New Musical' at the Olivier Awards. It is based in the Park Hall Estate in which city?

6. How many times was the Australian F1 Grand Prix red flagged?

7. Which airport becomes the second, after Teeside, to scrap the 100ml rule for liquids, courtesy of new scanning technology?

8. What was significant about the Project CAV Forth bus service in Edinburgh?

9. How many felony charges of falsifying business records in the first degree did Donald Trump face after appearing in a Manhattan court early in the month?

10. Who won the US Masters golf tournament?

11. It was announced that there would be filming of ITV's I'm a Celebrity, All Stars. In which country?

12. Present as an April Fool's joke until April 10th, which well known landmark had a tenth scale replica appear in close proximity?

13. Who did England's Womens football team defeat on penalties to win the first ever Finalissima?

14. Which country officially joined NATO?

15. Former *Chancellor of the Exchequer,* Nigel Lawson sadly passed away. He was also known as Baron Lawson of Blaby. Which English city is Blaby a district of?

16. Which movie broke box office records, scoring the most successful global opening of all time for an animated film. Overtaking the previous holder *Frozen 2*?

17. A BBC Radio 2 show revealed Bohemian Rhapsody as *Your Ultimate Queen Song* following a listener vote to discover the nation's favourite Queen song. What was in 2nd place?

18. *Air Force One* is a military version of which type of airliner?

19. What type of newly created emoji displayed on X (formerly) Twitter for various Coronation related hashtags?

20. Which star of *Stranger Things* announced she is engaged to Jake Bongiovi, her boyfriend of two-and-a-half years?

21. In Switzerland, Easter Eggs are not delivered by a bunny but by which other creature?

22. Which horse won the Grand National at Aintree?

23. Who became the newest judge on the latest series of Britain's Got Talent?

24. Who were the first EFL League One team to be relegated in season 2022/23?

25. Brendan Moore, Olivier Marteel and Leo Scullion are referees in which sport?

26. The BBC reported that US President Joe Biden would not be attending King Charles' Coronation. Who attended in his place?

27. The RSPB published the year's Big Garden Birdwatch list. How many of the top 10 can you name?

28. Which National Park changed its name to Bannau Brycheiniog?
29. The most powerful rocket ever built had its launch called off at the last minute by its Space X project company. What is the name of the rocket?
30. The Royal Mail released a new set of stamps. Their theme was about 'The Legend of' which person?
31. Which two broadcasters were named as Radio 2's presenters for the Eurovision Final?
32. Which recording artist was in the Number 1 spot of both the UK singles and albums charts on April 19th?
33. Which football team were the first to be relegated from League 2 in the 2022/23 season?
34. Sadly, Barry Humphries passed away this month. What was the name of Dame Edna Everage's bridesmaid and constant companion?
35. Who won this year's mens London Marathon?
36. Who replaced Dominic Raab as Deputy Prime Minister?
37. The UK government tested its Emergency Alarm System on Sunday 23 April. At what time was the alert issued?
38. US President Joe Biden announced his intention to contest the next presidential election. How old was he on January 1st 2023?
39. Lewis Capaldi went straight in to the Number One spot on the UK Official Singles Chart in late April. With which song?
40. A special programme was shown on BBC2 to celebrate a landmark anniversary of University Challenge. How old is the series?
41. Which of Freddie Mercury's oldest friends announced they were putting many of his personal treasures bequeathed to them up for auction in September?

42. It was announced that Len Goodman had sadly passed away. Aside from being Head Judge on Strictly Come Dancing, he also held the post on the United States version of the show. What is it called?

43. Stuart Field from Sheffield became 2023 champion of which television competition?

44. Which Labour Party MP had the whip suspended following a letter in the Observer newspaper?

45. This last F1 Grand Prix to be held in April was held in Baku. In which country is this?

April 2023 - Answers

1. After Antonio Conté left Tottenham Hotspur, which two Premier League football clubs sacked their managers/head coaches at the start of April? **Chelsea and Leicester City**

2. Sadly, Paul O'Grady passed away. What was the name of his Television and Stage drag persona? **Lily Savage**

3. Which European country was the subject of King Charles First State visit? **Germany**

4. An investigation conducted by the Information Commissioner's Office (ICO) found which popular video sharing app breached data protection law and fined it £12.7 million? **Tik Tok**

5. *Standing at the Sky's Edge* won 'Best New Musical' at the Olivier Awards. It is based in the Park Hall Estate in which city? **Sheffield**

6. How many times was the Australian F1 Grand Prix red flagged? **3**

7. Which airport becomes the second, after Teeside, to scrap the 100ml rule for liquids, courtesy of new scanning technology? **London City**

8. What was significant about the Project CAVForth bus service in Edinburgh? **It was set to be the World's first full-size, self driving bus service.**

9. How many felony charges of falsifying business records in the first degree does Donald Trump face after appearing in a Manhattan court early in the month? **34**

10. Who won the US Masters golf tournament? **John Rahm**

11. It was announced that there would be filming of ITV's I'm a Celebrity, All Stars. In which country? **South Africa**

12. Present as an April Fool's joke until April 10th, which well known landmark had a tenth scale replica appear in close proximity? **The Eiffel Tower**

13. Who did England's womens football team defeat on penalties to win the first ever Finalissima? **Brazil**

14. Which country officially joined NATO? **Finland**

15. Former *Chancellor of the Exchequer,* Nigel Lawson sadly passed away. He was also known as Baron Lawson of Blaby. Which English city is Blaby a district of? **Leicester**

16. Which movie broke box office records, scoring the most successful global opening of all time for an animated film. Overtaking the previous holder *Frozen 2*? **Super Mario Bros.**

17. A BBC Radio 2 show revealed Bohemian Rhapsody as *Your Ultimate Queen Song* following a listener vote to discover the nation's favourite Queen song. What was in 2nd place? **Don't Stop Me Now**

18. *Air Force One* is a military version of which type of airliner? **Boeing 747**

19. What type of newly created emoji displayed on X (Formerly Twitter) for various Coronation related hashtags? **A Crown**

20. Which star of *Stranger Things* announced she is engaged to Jake Bongiovi, her boyfriend of two-and-a-half years? **Millie Bobby Brown**

21. In Switzerland, Easter Eggs are not delivered by a bunny but by which other creature? **A cuckoo**

22. Which horse won the Grand National at Aintree? **Corach Rambler**

23. Who became the newest judge on the latest series of Britain's Got Talent? **Bruno Tonioli**

24. Who were the first EFL League One team to be relegated in season 2022/23? **Forest Green Rovers**

25. Brendan Moore, Olivier Marteel and Leo Scullion are referees in which sport? **Snooker**

26. The BBC reported that US President Joe Biden would not be attending King Charles' Coronation. Who attended in his place? **The First Lady, Jill Biden**

27. The RSPB published the year's Big Garden Birdwatch list. How many of the top 10 can you name? **House Sparrow, Blue Tit, Starling, Woodpigeon, Blackbird, Robin, Goldfinch, Great Tit, Magpie, Long-Tailed Tit**

28. Which National Park changed its name to Bannau Brycheiniog? **The Brecon Beacons**

29. The most powerful rocket ever built had its launch called off at the last minute by its Space X project company. What is the name of the rocket? **Starship**

30. The Royal Mail released a new set of stamps. Their theme was about 'The Legend of' which person? **Robin Hood**

31. Which two broadcasters were named as Radio 2's presenters for the Eurovision Final? **Scott Mills and Rylan Clark**

32. Which recording artist was in the Number 1 spot of both the UK singles and albums charts on April 19th? **Ellie Goulding**

33. Which football team were the first to be relegated from League 2 in the 2022/23 season? **Rochdale FC**

34. Sadly, Barry Humphries passed away this month. What was the name of Dame Edna Everage's bridesmaid and constant companion? **Madge Allsop**

35. Who won this year's mens London Marathon? **Kelvin Kiptum**

36. Who replaced Dominic Raab as Deputy Prime Minister? **Oliver Dowden**

37. The UK government tested its Emergency Alarm System on Sunday 23 April. At what time was the alert issued? **3Pm**

38. US President Joe Biden announced his intention to contest the next presidential election. How old was he on January 1st 2023? **80**

39. Lewis Capaldi went straight in to the Number One spot on the UK Official Singles Chart in late April. With which song? **Wish you the Best**

40. A special programme was shown on BBC2 to celebrate a landmark anniversary of University Challenge. How old is the series? **Sixty Years**

41. Which of Freddie Mercury's oldest friends announced they were putting many of his personal treasures bequeathed to them up for auction in September? **Mary Austin**

42. It was announced that Len Goodman had sadly passed away. Aside from being Head Judge on Strictly Come Dancing, he also held the post on the United States version of the show. What is it called? **Dancing with the Stars**

43. Stuart Field from Sheffield became 2023 champion of which television competition? **Mastermind**

44. Which Labour Party MP had the whip suspended following a letter in the Observer newspaper? **Diane Abbott**

45. This last F1 Grand Prix to be held in April was held in Baku. In which country is this? **Azerbaijan**

May 2023 - Questions

1. Who was the theme of this year's Met Gala?
2. Which country did this year's World Snooker Champion come from?
3. The Prince and Princess of Wales celebrated their Wedding Anniversary, how many years have they been married?
4. Who was the chairman of the BBC who resigned following the findings of the Heppinstall enquiry?
5. Which actress won her High Court case over her fee for a Sci-fi film that was never made?
6. Which EFL Championship team secured automatic promotion to the Premier League following a 2-0 defeat of West Bromwich Albion?
7. 'Til next time take care of yourselves and each other' was a catchphrase associated with which TV host who sadly, passed away in May?
8. Arnold George Dorsey MBE celebrated his 87th birthday. By what name is this singer better known?
9. Which duo who originally started recording together in the 1980's had a new album in the charts called *Fuse*?
10. According to United Nations figures, which country has overtaken China as the most populated?
11. Which superhero team hit local cinemas this month with their third film - Vol 3?
12. Which chart topping band reunited after 36 years to perform at the opening of Eurovision Week 2023?
13. Which famous actor released their first novel entitled; *The Making of Another Major Motion Picture Masterpiece*?

14. What sort of items were carried by Penny Mordaunt during the Coronation Ceremony?
15. The English National Opera narrowed down its search for a new home to five cities. Can you name them?
16. Tedros Adhanom Ghebreyesus made a statement that the COVID-19 Global health emergency is over but people should remain cautious. In making this announcement, which body was he Director General of?
17. Which EFL League One team secured the title following a defeat of Port Vale?
18. Scientists named a new group of butterflies after which Lord of the Rings villain?
19. Which country have built the world's first *charge as you drive* motorway?
20. What type of dish was declared the Coronation's official party food?
21. How many original members of Take That performed at the Coronation Concert?
22. Which actor confirmed that, at the age of 79, he had become a father for the seventh time?
23. Last year AJ Odudu announced the 12 points awarded by the UK Jury at Eurovision. Who did so this year?
24. Which 4 teams made it to the playoff stages of EFL League 2?
25. Which country's entry scored the most points from the viewer vote part of the 2023 Eurovision Song Contest?
26. What type of aircraft toured every Lincolnshire RAF Bomber Command base to mark the 80th anniversary of the *Dambusters* raids?
27. In the TV comedy series *Colin from Accounts*, who or what is Colin?

28. Who presented, Ben Francis, founder of Gymshark with his MBE?
29. Who was recalled to the England Cricket Test Squad for the first time since breaking his leg last August?
30. The Department for Transport (DfT) announced that which Rail company's contract would not be renewed on 28 May 2023?
31. Which TV programme won the BAFTA for *Best Soap and Continuing Drama*?
32. Which country's Presidential Election reached a run off stage between current President Recep Tayyip Erdogan and Kemal Kilicdaroglu?
33. In which sport did London Lions beat Leicester Riders to win their leagues play-off title?
34. What kind of scientists were interested in an event called *AT2021lwx* in May? A: Astronomers, B: Botanists C: Meteorologists D: Paleontologists
35. On 17th May, it was reported that which former French President had lost his appeal against a prison sentence for corruption?
36. In which city was the G7 Summit held in May?
37. The hippopotamus, walrus, narwhal, killer whale and sperm whale were the subject of an attempt by the UK government to extend an Act making it illegal to trade which material?
38. The city of Catania was subjected to precipitation of volcanic ash following the eruption of which volcano?
39. Who won the PGA Golf Championship?
40. Which musical with the additional title; *Idiots Assemble,* began a London West End run at The Phoenix Theatre?
41. Where did the 2023 Giro D'Italia finish, having started on May 6th in Fossacesia?

42. Bobi, the world's oldest dog celebrated their birthday in style, with more than 100 guests. How old is Bobi?

43. Which 4 darts players qualified for the 2023 Cazoo Premier League Play-Offs?

44. Which member of the Royal Family surprised a group of schoolchildren with their visit to The Chelsea Flower Show?

45. Which basketball team from Denver reached the NBA finals for the first time in their history?

46. Where did Radio 1's Big Weekend music festival take place?

47. Steve Coogan, Lee Mack and Paul Whitehouse joined a rally against sewage pollution at which British body of water?

48. Who scored Everton's winning goal to beat AFC Bournemouth thus avoiding relegation at the expense of Leicester City?

49. Which long established Heavy Rock band had a new album release with the London Philharmonic Orchestra called *Drastic Symphonies*?

50. It was announced that the character of Charlie Fairhead was set for a final exit from the TV Drama *Casualty*. Which actor plays the role?

51. Who did Saracens beat in the Gallagher Premiership Final?

52. Protests took place in Central London against plans to extend the ULEZ. What does the acronym ULEZ stand for?

53. In mens cricket who won the Indian Premier League in a last ball thriller?

54. It was announced that, sadly, Tina Turner passed away at the age of 83. What is the name she was given at birth?

55. Who became the new president of the RSPCA?

May 2023 - Answers

1. Who was the theme of this year's Met Gala? **Karl Lagerfeld**
2. Which country did this year's World Snooker Champion come from? **Belgium**
3. The Prince and Princess of Wales celebrated their Wedding Anniversary, how many years have they been married? **12**
4. Who was the chairman of the BBC who resigned following the findings of the Heppinstall enquiry? **Richard Sharp**
5. Which actress won her High Court case over her fee for a Sci-fi film that was never made? **Eva Green**
6. Which EFL Championship team secured automatic promotion to the Premier League following a 2-0 defeat of West Bromwich Albion? **Sheffield United**
7. 'Til next time take care of yourselves and each other' was a catchphrase associated with which TV host who sadly, passed away in May? **Jerry Springer**
8. Arnold George Dorsey MBE celebrated his 87th birthday. By what name is this singer better known? **Englebert Humperdinck**
9. Which duo who originally started recording together in the 1980's had a new album in the charts called *Fuse*? **Everything But the Girl (Ben Watt and Tracy Thorn)**
10. According to United Nations figures, which country has overtaken China as the most populated? **India**
11. Which superhero team hit local cinemas this month with their third film - Vol 3? **Guardians of the Galaxy**
12. Which chart topping band reunited after 36 years to perform at the opening of Eurovision Week 2023? **Frankie Goes to Hollywood**

13. Which famous actor released their first novel entitled; *The Making of Another Major Motion Picture Masterpiece*? **Tom Hanks**

14. What sort of items were carried by Penny Mordaunt during the Coronation Ceremony? **Swords**

15. The English National Opera narrowed down its search for a new home to five cities. Can you name them? **Birmingham, Bristol, Manchester, Liverpool and Nottingham**

16. Tedros Adhanom Ghebreyesus made a statement that the COVID-19 Global health emergency is over but people should remain cautious. In making this announcement, which body was he Director General of? **The World Health Organisation**

17. Which EFL League One team secured the title following a defeat of Port Vale? **Plymouth Argyle**

18. Scientists named a new group of butterflies after which Lord of the Rings villain? **Sauron**

19. Which country have built the world's first *charge as you drive* motorway? **Sweden**

20. What type of dish was declared the Coronation's official party food? **Quiche**

21. How many original members of Take That performed at the Coronation Concert? **Three**

22. Which actor confirmed that, at the age of 79, he had become a father for the seventh time? **Robert De Niro**

23. Last year AJ Odudu announced the 12 points awarded by the UK Jury at Eurovision. Who did so this year? **Catherine Tate**

24. Which 4 teams made it to the playoff stages of EFL League 2? **Bradford City, Carlisle United, Salford City and Stockport County**

25. Which country's entry scored the most points from the viewer vote part of the 2023 Eurovision Song Contest? **Finland**

26. What type of aircraft toured every Lincolnshire RAF Bomber Command base to mark the 80th anniversary of the *Dambusters* raids? **A Lancaster**

27. In the TV comedy series *Colin from Accounts*, who or what is Colin? **A Dog**

28. Who presented, Ben Francis, founder of Gymshark with his MBE? **Prince William**

29. Who was recalled to the England Cricket Test Squad for the first time since breaking his leg last August? **Jonny Bairstow**

30. The Department for Transport (DfT) announced that which Rail company's contract would not be renewed on 28 May 2023? **First TransPennine Express Limited (TransPennine Express)**

31. Which TV programme won the BAFTA for *Best Soap and Continuing Drama*? **Casualty**

32. Which country's Presidential Election reached a run off stage between current President Recep Tayyip Erdogan and Kemal Kilicdaroglu? **Turkey**

33. In which sport did London Lions beat Leicester Riders to win their leagues play-off title? **Basketball**

34. What kind of scientists were interested in an event called *AT2021lwx* in May? A: Astronomers, B: Botanists C: Meteorologists D: Paleontologists **A (it is the biggest observed explosion in space)**

35. On 17th May, it was reported that which former French President had lost his appeal against a prison sentence for corruption? **Nicolas Sarkozy**

36. In which city was the G7 Summit held in May? **Hiroshima, Japan**

37. The hippopotamus, walrus, narwhal, killer whale and sperm whale were the subject of an attempt by the UK government

to extend an Act making it illegal to trade which material? **Ivory**

38. The city of Catania was subjected to precipitation of volcanic ash following the eruption of which volcano? **Mount Etna**

39. Who won the PGA Golf Championship? **Brooks Koepka**

40. Which musical with the additional title; *Idiots Assemble,* began a London West End run at The Phoenix Theatre? **Spitting Image, The Musical**

41. Where did the 2023 Giro D'Italia finish, having started on May 6th in Fossacesia? **Rome**

42. Bobi, the world's oldest dog celebrated their birthday in style, with more than 100 guests. How old is Bobi? **31**

43. Which 4 darts players qualified for the 2023 Cazoo Premier League Play-Offs? **Johnny Clayton, Gerwyn Price, Michael Smith and Michael Van Gerwen**

44. Which member of the Royal Family surprised a group of schoolchildren with their visit to The Chelsea Flower Show? **Kate Middleton, Princess of Wales**

45. Which basketball team from Denver reached the NBA finals for the first time in their history? **Denver Nuggets**

46. Where did Radio 1's Big Weekend music festival take place? **Dundee**

47. Steve Coogan, Lee Mack and Paul Whitehouse joined a rally against sewage pollution at which British body of water? **Lake Windermere**

48. Who scored Everton's winning goal to beat AFC Bournemouth thus avoiding relegation at the expense of Leicester City? **Abdoulaye Doucoure**

49. Which long established Heavy Rock band had a new album release with the London Philharmonic Orchestra called *Drastic Symphonies*? **Def Leppard**

50. It was announced that the character of Charlie Fairhead was set for a final exit from the TV Drama *Casualty*. Which actor plays the role? **Derek Thompson**

51. Who did Saracens beat in the Gallagher Premiership Final? **Sale Sharks**

52. Protests took place in Central London against plans to extend the ULEZ. What does the acronym ULEZ stand for? **Ultra Low Emission Zone**

53. In mens cricket who won the Indian Premier League in a last ball thriller? **Chennai Super Kings**

54. It was announced that, sadly, Tina Turner passed away at the age of 83. What is the name she was given at birth? **Anna Mae Bullock**

55. Who became the new president of the RSPCA? **Chris Packham**

June 2023 - Questions

1. What did Norwegian, Viggo Venn win?
2. Which Scottish Premier League team staged a notable comeback to win their play off tie against Patrick Thistle?
3. Which of these newspapers is not owned by Reach plc? A: Daily Express, B: Daily Mail, C: Daily Mirror or D: Daily Star
4. In the early June test match, who took 5 wickets in Ireland's 2nd innings on his debut for England
5. Which band formed in the 1960's by two brothers had a new album in the UK top ten called *The Girl is Crying in Her Latte*?
6. Who was the Vice President to Donald Trump who announced they will compete against him for the Republican Party's Presidential nomination
7. Which Rugby Club were suspended from the Premiership early this month?
8. Which programme won *Best Soap* at the 2023 British Soap awards?
9. Roland Garros, home of the French Open Tennis has 3 named show courts. Two are Court Philippe Chatrier and Court Simonne Mathieu. What is the other called?
10. Which famous locomotive featured in pictures of King Charles' visit to Pickering as it pulled the royal train on the North Yorkshire Moors Railway?
11. In which country did Manchester City win the Champions League Final?
12. In which country's rainforest did rescue teams find 4 children who were missing after having survived a light aircraft crash for nearly six weeks?

13. Which rider won his home Italian Moto GP on a Ducati at Mugello?
14. Boris Johnson wrote a new newspaper column which appeared in which publication?
15. Which tennis player overtook Emma Raducanu as GB's number one in June?
16. Which streaming service was reported to have mutually agreed to end its deal with the Duke and Duchess of Sussex?
17. Which manufacturers won the Le Mans 24 hr race?
18. Which Milan football team was owned for many years by the late Silvio Berlusconi?
19. In which county is Stonehenge where people gathered to welcome the Summer Solstice?
20. When playing test cricket, what number does England captain Ben Stokes have on the back of his shirt?
21. The final movie in the Indiana Jones series premiered in London. What is its title?
22. Which actor from the cast of *Line of Duty* was awarded an MBE in recognition of her work on dementia?
23. Who scored a hat-trick for England in their 7-0 defeat of North Macedonia?
24. Who was crowned Masterchef UK champion, becoming the 19th champion to hold the title?
25. The F1 Canadian Grand Prix saw an anniversary of the first time a safety car was used in such a competition. Was it A: 20 years ago, B: 30 years ago, C: 40 years ago or D: 50 years ago?
26. Who was announced to be taking over from Rylan Clark as co-host of *Strictly It Takes Two* when it recommences in September?

27. Which artist saw their album *The Show* enter the UK Top 100 Album Chart at Number One?
28. Who won the US Open mens golf tournament?
29. Max Park was reported to have broken the record to solve the 3 x 3 x 3 Rubiks Cube. To the nearest second, is it A: 3s, B: 13s, C: 23s or D: 33s?
30. The giant mechanical bull from last years Commonwealth Games has been given a name after a public vote chose it to be named after which rock legend?
31. Where did the England Women's team lose the test match game which began the Ashes Series contest?
32. Which member of the Royal Family launched the Homewards campaign, visiting housing and training projects at Lambeth, Bournemouth and Newport?
33. Zharnel Hughes set a new British record for the 100m sprint, beating the previous time set 30 years ago by which athlete?
34. Which popular radio quiz made its debut as a television version on More 4?
35. In addition to ownership of Wrexham FC, Ryan Reynolds and Rob McElhenney were reported to have invested in which Formula One team?
36. Which two Major League Baseball teams contested the London Series?
37. Which country brought in a new law to align the nation's two traditional age-counting methods with international standards?
38. Which jockey won the Ascot Gold Cup riding *Courage Mon Ami*?
39. Which music artist has joined others including footballer Wilfried Zaha to takeover the running of AFC Croydon?
40. Which water utilities company was the subject of reported concerns about its ability to continue operating without a

multi-billion cash injection and then fined 3.3 million for sewage pollution?

June 2023 - Answers

1. What did Norwegian, Viggo Venn win? **Britain's Got Talent**

2. Which Scottish Premier League team staged a notable comeback to win their play off tie against Patrick Thistle? **Ross County**

3. Which of these newspapers is not owned by Reach plc? A: Daily Express, B: Daily Mail, C: Daily Mirror or D: Daily Star **B**

4. In the early June test match, who took 5 wickets in Ireland's 2nd innings on his debut for England? **Josh Tongue**

5. Which band formed in the 1960's by two brothers had a new album in the UK top ten called *The Girl is Crying in Her Latte*? **Sparks**

6. Who was the Vice President to Donald Trump who announced they will compete against him for the Republican Party's Presidential nomination **Mike Pence**

7. Which Rugby Club were suspended from the Premiership early this month? **London Irish**

8. Which programme won *Best Soap* at the 2023 British Soap awards? **Eastenders**

9. Roland Garros, home of the French Open Tennis has 3 named show courts. Two are Court Philippe Chatrier and Court Simonne Mathieu. What is the other called? **Court Suzanne Lenglen**

10. Which famous locomotive featured in pictures of King Charles' visit to Pickering as it pulled the royal train on the North Yorkshire Moors Railway? **The Flying Scotsman**

11. In which country did Manchester City win the Champions League Final? **Turkey**

12. In which country's rainforest did rescue teams find 4 children who were missing after having survived a light aircraft crash for nearly six weeks? **Colombia**

13. Which rider won his home Italian Moto GP on a Ducati at Mugello? **Francesco Bagnaia**

14. Boris Johnson wrote a new newspaper column which appeared in which publication? **The Daily Mail**

15. Which tennis player overtook Emma Raducanu as GB's number one in June? **Katie Boulter**

16. Which streaming service was reported to have mutually agreed to end its deal with the Duke and Duchess of Sussex? **Spotify**

17. Which manufacturers won the Le Mans 24 hr race? **Ferrari**

18. Which Milan football team was owned for many years by the late Silvio Berlusconi? **AC Milan**

19. In which county is Stonehenge where people gathered to welcome the Summer Solstice? **Wiltshire**

20. When playing test cricket, what number does England captain Ben Stokes have on the back of his shirt? **55**

21. The final movie in the Indiana Jones series premiered in London. What is its title? **Indiana Jones and the Dial of Destiny**

22. Which actor from the cast of *Line of Duty* was awarded an MBE in recognition of her work on dementia? **Vicky McLure**

23. Who scored a hat-trick for England in their 7-0 defeat of North Macedonia? **Bukayo Saka**

24. Who was crowned Masterchef UK champion, becoming the 19th champion to hold the title? **Chariya Khattiyot**

25. The F1 Canadian Grand Prix saw an anniversary of the first time a safety car was used in such a competition. Was it A: 20 years ago, B: 30 years ago, C: 40 years ago or D: 50 years ago? **D**

26. Who was announced to be taking over from Rylan Clark as co-host of *Strictly It Takes Two* when it recommences in September? **Fleur East**

27. Which artist saw their album *The Show* enter the UK Top 100 Album Chart at Number One? **Niall Horan**

28. Who won the US Open mens golf tournament? **Wyndham Clark**

29. Max Park was reported to have broken the record to solve the 3 x 3 x 3 Rubiks Cube. To the nearest second, is it A: 3s, B: 13s, C: 23s or D: 33s? **A**

30. The giant mechanical bull from last years Commonwealth Games has been given a name after a public vote chose it to be named after which rock legend? **Ozzy Osbourne**

31. Where did the England Women's team lose the test match game which began the Ashes Series contest? **Trent Bridge**

32. Which member of the Royal Family launched the Homewards campaign, visiting housing and training projects at Lambeth, Bournemouth and Newport? **Prince William, Prince of Wales**

33. Zharnel Hughes set a new British record for the 100m sprint, beating the previous time set 30 years ago by which athlete? **Linford Christie**

34. Which popular radio quiz made its debut as a television version on More 4? **Popmaster**

35. In addition to ownership of Wrexham FC, Ryan Reynolds and Rob McElhenney were reported to have invested in which Formula One team? **Alpine**

36. Which two Major League Baseball teams contested the London Series? **Chicago Cubs and St Louis Cardinals**

37. Which country brought in a new law to align the nation's two traditional age-counting methods with international standards? **South Korea**

38. Which jockey won the Ascot Gold Cup riding *Courage Mon Ami*? **Frankie Dettori**

39. Which music artist has joined others including footballer Wilfried Zaha to takeover the running of AFC Croydon? **Stormzy**

40. Which water utilities company was the subject of reported concerns about its ability to continue operating without a multi-billion cash injection and then fined 3.3 million for sewage pollution? **Thames Water**

July 2023 - Questions

1. What award did Grayson Perry receive in a ceremony at Windsor Castle? A: MBE, B: OBE C: CBE, D: Knighthood

2. Which fielder controversially stumped England's Jonny Bairstow in the second Ashes test match at Lord's?

3. Which GB News presenter broadcast his concerns about being denied the opportunity to operate a bank account?

4. Which major Spanish city saw the beginning stage of the 2023 Tour de France?

5. The NHS marked a special anniversary. How many years has it been in existence? A: 75, B: 100, C: 125 or D: 150

6. Which singer followed up their appearance at Glastonbury by achieving Number One on the UK Album Chart with *The Good Witch*?

7. It was reported that Ant and Dec were to reboot *Byker Grove* in a new TV venture. What were their characters names when they last appeared in the original series 30 years ago?

8. King Charles III visited Scotland for ceremonial celebrations marking the coronation. In which city did these take place? A: Inverness, B: Edinburgh, C: Perth, D: Glasgow

9. Which EFL League Two club named Hannah Dingley as their new caretaker boss, making her the first woman to manage a professional men's team in English football?

10. Who was the highest placed British driver at the F1 British Grand Prix at Silverstone?

11. Which popular motor car ceased production after more than 4 decades of manufacturing?

12. Which tennis player defeated Andy Murray in the Gentleman's Singles at Wimbledon?

13. Prime Minister Mark Rutte has said he will quit politics after which country's coalition government collapsed?

14. Who hit the winning runs to give England their win in the 3rd Ashes Test at Headingly?

15. Easyjet confirmed it had cancelled 1,700 flights between July to September to and from which UK airport?

16. The Mount Fagradalsfjall volcano began erupting. In which country is it?

17. It was reported that in the week since it's launch, Facebook owner Meta signed up more than 100 million users to new social media app. What is it called?

18. The Isle of Man, Isle of Wight, Ynys Mon, Jersey, Guernsey, Alderney, Sark, Orkney, The Western Islands and The Shetland Isles had teams at this year's Island Games, but which of these was also the host?

19. Who saved a last minute penalty kick to ensure the England Football team won the final of the European Under 21 Championship?

20. Which band were added to the Reading and Leeds festival bill after Lewis Capaldi announced a break from touring?

21. Which golf course was announced as the venue for the 2026 British Open?

22. Which F1 racing driver was announced as a replacement for Nyck de Vries at the Alpha Tauri team?

23. With the news full of statistics about record breaking high temperatures. What, to the nearest whole figure, is 40 degrees Celsius in degrees Fahrenheit?

24. Who was the last tennis player to defeat Novak Djokovic in a singles match on Wimbledon Centre Court before Carlos Alcaraz did so in this years final?

25. Who announced in July that they were quitting their role as Government Defence Secretary?

26. Who were the two beaten semi-finalists at the Cricket Vitality T20 Blast Finals Day contested at Edgbaston?

27. The Royal tradition of *Swan Upping* took place in July. On which body of water is it conducted?

28. Which club did Declan Rice join after his transfer from West Ham United?

29. Jaguar Land Rover-owner Tata confirmed plans to build its flagship electric car battery factory in which UK county?

30. Who plays the title role in the *Barbie* movie?

31. Which Australian State withdrew from its role of host for the 2026 Commonwealth Games?

32. Olivia Rodrigo entered the UK Singles Chart at Number 2 in July with what title?

33. Three countries were represented at the FIFA Women's World Cup Final 32 who had never been successful in reaching a Men's World Cup Finals Stage. One of these was The Philippines. Which are the other two?

34. Which Social Media site, replaced its long standing logo with an 'X' ?

35. Which candidate successfully held the seat of Uxbridge and South Ruislip for the Conservative Party at a by-election?

36. Spotify raised its premium subscription price for millions. In which European country was it founded in 2006?

37. The poor Manchester weather saw to it that the 4th Ashes test ended in a draw. How many runs did England score in their first and only innings of the match? A: 389 B: 490 C: 592 D: 643

38. A World War One German U-boat was identified by divers off the coast of which British islands?

39. The River Seine is being cleaned in time for next years Summer Olympics. For how many years has swimming there been

banned because of the levels of water pollution that could make people ill? A:25 B: 50 C: 75 D: 100

40. What became the first spirit drink to be afforded protected status under the UKGI scheme?

41. The *Oppenheimer* movie was released on British cinema screens. Who directed it?

42. Sadly, Singer Tony Bennett passed away aged 96. Which song did he take to the top of the UK Singles Chart in 1953?

43. By how many strokes did Brian Harman lead the rest of the field as he won the British Open Golf 2023?

44. Which horse narrowly beat *Westover* by a head where a class field contested the King George VI and Queen Elizabeth QIPCO Stakes at Ascot?

45. Boris Johnson's planning permission for a new swimming pool were put on hold over concerns for the environmental impact on which creatures?

July 2023 - Answers

1. What award did Grayson Perry receive in a ceremony at Windsor Castle? A: MBE, B: OBE C: CBE, D: Knighthood **D**

2. Which fielder controversially stumped England's Jonny Bairstow in the second Ashes test match at Lord's? **Alex Carey**

3. Which GB News presenter broadcast his concerns about being denied the opportunity to operate a bank account? **Nigel Farage**

4. Which major Spanish city saw the beginning stage of the 2023 Tour de France? **Bilbao**

5. The NHS marked a special anniversary. How many years has it been in existence? A: 75, B: 100, C: 125 or D: 150 **A**

6. Which singer followed up their appearance at Glastonbury by achieving Number One on the UK Album Chart with *The Good Witch*? **Maisie Peters**

7. It was reported that Ant and Dec were to reboot *Byker Grove* in a new TV venture. What were their characters names when they last appeared in the original series 30 years ago? **PJ and Duncan**

8. King Charles III visited Scotland for ceremonial celebrations marking the coronation. In which city did these take place? A: Inverness, B: Edinburgh, C: Perth, D: Glasgow **B**

9. Which EFL League Two club named Hannah Dingley as their new caretaker boss, making her the first woman to manage a professional men's team in English football? **Forest Green Rovers**

10. Who was the highest placed British driver at the F1 British Grand Prix at Silverstone? **Lando Norris**

11. Which popular motor car ceased production after more than 4 decades of manufacturing? **Ford Fiesta**

12. Which tennis player defeated Andy Murray in the Gentleman's Singles at Wimbledon? **Stefano Tsitsipas**

13. Prime Minister Mark Rutte has said he will quit politics after which country's coalition government collapsed? **The Netherlands**

14. Who hit the winning runs to give England their win in the 3rd Ashes Test at Headingly? **Chris Woakes**

15. Easyjet confirmed it had cancelled 1,700 flights between July to September to and from which UK airport? **London Gatwick**

16. The Mount Fagradalsfjall volcano began erupting. In which country is it? **Iceland**

17. It was reported that in the week since it's launch, Facebook owner Meta signed up more than 100 million users to new social media app. What is it called? **Threads**

18. The Isle of Man, Isle of Wight, Ynys Mon, Jersey, Guernsey, Alderney, Sark, Orkney, The Western Islands and The Shetland Isles had teams at this year's Island Games, but which of these was also the host? **Guernsey**

19. Who saved a last minute penalty kick to ensure the England Football team won the final of the European Under 21 Championship? **James Trafford**

20. Which band were added to the Reading and Leeds festival bill after Lewis Capaldi announced a break from touring? **The 1975**

21. Which golf course was announced as the venue for the 2026 British Open? **Royal Birkdale**

22. Which F1 racing driver was announced as a replacement for Nyck de Vries at the Alpha Tauri team? **Daniel Ricciardo**

23. With the news full of statistics about record breaking high temperatures. What, to the nearest whole figure, is 40 degrees Celsius in degrees Fahrenheit? **104F**

24. Who was the last tennis player to defeat Novak Djokovic in a singles match on Wimbledon Centre Court before Carlos Alcaraz did so in this years final? **Andy Murray**

25. Who announced in July that they were quitting their role as Government Defence Secretary? **Ben Wallace**

26. Who were the two beaten semi-finalists at the Cricket Vitality T20 Blast Finals Day contested at Edgbaston? **Hampshire and Surrey**

27. The Royal tradition of *Swan Upping* took place in July. On which body of water is it conducted? **The River Thames**

28. Which club did Declan Rice join after his transfer from West Ham United? **Arsenal**

29. Jaguar Land Rover-owner Tata confirmed plans to build its flagship electric car battery factory in which UK county? **Somerset**

30. Who plays the title role in the *Barbie* movie? **Margot Robbie**

31. Which Australian State withdrew from its role of host for the 2026 Commonwealth Games? **Victoria**

32. Olivia Rodrigo entered the UK Singles Chart at Number 2 in July with what title? **Vampire**

33. Three countries were represented at the FIFA Women's World Cup Final 32 who had never been successful in reaching a Men's World Cup Finals Stage. One of these was The Philippines. Which are the other two? **Vietnam and Zambia**

34. Which Social Media site, replaced its long standing logo with an 'X' ? **Twitter**

35. Which candidate successfully held the seat of Uxbridge and South Ruislip for the Conservative Party at a by-election? **Steve Tuckwell**

36. Spotify raised its premium subscription price for millions. In which European country was it founded in 2006? **Sweden**

37. The poor Manchester weather saw to it that the 4th Ashes test ended in a draw. How many runs did England score in their first and only innings of the match? A: 389 B: 490 C: 592 D: 643 **C**

38. A World War One German U-boat was identified by divers off the coast of which British islands? **Shetland**

39. The River Seine is being cleaned in time for next years Summer Olympics. For how many years has swimming there been banned because of the levels of water pollution that could make people ill? A:25 B: 50 C: 75 D: 100 **D**

40. What became the first spirit drink to be afforded protected status under the UKGI scheme? **Welsh Whiskey**

41. The *Oppenheimer* movie was released on British cinema screens. Who directed it? **Christopher Nolan**

42. Sadly, Singer Tony Bennett passed away aged 96. Which song did he take to the top of the UK Singles Chart in 1953? **Stranger in Paradise**

43. By how many strokes did Brian Harman lead the rest of the field as he won the British Open Golf 2023? **Six**

44. Which horse narrowly beat *Westover* by a head where a class field contested the King George VI and Queen Elizabeth QIPCO Stakes at Ascot? **Hukum**

45. Boris Johnson's planning permission for a new swimming pool were put on hold over concerns for the environmental impact on which creatures? **Newts**

August 2023 - Questions

1. Who took a wicket with the final ball of his professional cricket playing career to take the Ashes series to a 2-2 draw?
2. Which member of *The Rolling Stones* celebrated his 80th Birthday?
3. Which team announced that Formula 1 team principal Otmar Szafnauer is leaving them?
4. NASA managed to re establish contact with which spacecraft after a period of silence? Now 12 billion miles away from Earth, it was launched in 1977.
5. How many goals in total did England score in their Group D matches at the FIFA Women's World Cup?
6. Sadly, Sinead O'Connor passed away in August. What was her first UK Chart Single?
7. Who was the Host Nation of the Netball World Cup 2023?
8. While Rishi Sunak took a Summer Holiday in California, who was in charge of the country?
9. Which Olympic diving champion has said he will return to the pool after a two year break to target a spot at Paris 2024?
10. Britain's 'Wonkiest Pub' was controversially demolished following a fire. Where was it situated?
11. Which team put 7 goals past Port Vale in their opening match of the EFL League One Season?
12. How many people were in the honours list submitted by Liz Truss as an outgoing Prime Minister?
13. A World Scout Jamboree attracting more than 40,000 from 155 different countries was affected by a tropical storm. In which country was it scheduled?

14. After playing in the Ashes tests, Ben Duckett participated in *The Hundred.* Which team did he play for?

15. Who won the Netball World Cup 2023 tournament?

16. Members of Greenpeace staged a protest at the home of Rishi Sunak. In which county is his residence?

17. Filippo Ganna won gold at the World Cycling Championships in the Men's Individual Pursuit. Which country does he represent?

18. Who produced one of the most remarkable rounds in the history of golf, shooting 58 to win the LIV Golf Greenbrier title?

19. Asylum Seekers were evacuated from the Portland port barge they were housed in after evidence of Legionella bacteria was found in the water supply. What is the name of the barge?

20. After scoring against AFC Bournemouth, Mo Salah became Liverpool's 5th highest goal scorer. Can you name the 4 players above him?

21. What type of aircraft, the only one of its type not to have been fully restored, was flown this month to celebrate its 80th birthday?

22. Which England rugby union player was sent off during their 19-17 defeat of Wales at Twickenham?

23. It was reported that the Duke of Sussex has had their HRH removed on the royal family's website. This coincided with his visit to which country?

24. Who became the first woman batter to score a century in *The Hundred* competition?

25. Which music magazine's comeback issue sold out within minutes?

26. Who won their 36th Para-cycling gold at the Cycling World Championships in the C5 individual time trial?

27. An eight foot tall totem pole mysteriously appeared on a nature reserve overlooking the coast of which county?

28. The charity Guide Dogs UK suggested that a shortage of guide dogs might be mitigated by using more of which breed?

29. Which NFL legend became a minority owner in Birmingham City FC?

30. Who won the Women's Football World Cup Final?

31. Eight people were rescued from a cable car after one of the cables snapped leaving them stranded 900 feet above a ravine. In which country did this take place?

32. Le Touquet-Paris-Plage airport announced it was set to be renamed in honour of who?

33. It was reported that the UK's first ever transplant of which organ was carried out at the Churchill Hospital, Oxford last February?

34. In MotoGP, Francesco Bagnaia, won the feature race in Austria from pole, extending his world championship lead to 62 points. What is the name of the circuit where this took place?

35. Why was Lorna Rose Treen in the news this August?

36. Zharnel Hughes won a bronze medal at the World Athletics Championships in the 100m. Which country hosted the event?

37. Several songs from *Barbie the Album* featured on this August's UK Singles Chat. Which artist performed 'Dance The Night' ?

38. Harry Brook scored 105 in 42 balls but could not stop his team falling to defeat against Welsh Fire in *The Hundred*. Which team did he play for?

39. Who was announced to be taking over the presenter's role on the BBC programme *Inside the Factory*?

40. In August, Japan began its controversial discharge of treated waste water from which nuclear plant into the Pacific Ocean?

41. Can you name the 4 Arsenal players named in the PFA Men's Team of the Year?

42. Donald Trump became the first ever former US President to have a 'mugshot' taken. In which US State did this take place?

43. Who won the Silver medal in the Women's Pole Vault at the World Athletics Championships?

44. Which country became the first to successfully land a spacecraft near the South Pole of The Moon?

45. Over one hundred volunteers took part in a search for the *Loch Ness Monster*. Loch Ness is the biggest loch in Scotland by volume, but second in surface area to which other?

46. Which Rugby Union International side beat England for the first time ever at the end of August?

47. Which Rap star asked aspiring Republican presidential candidate Vivek Ramaswamy to stop using his songs?

48. Who won the 2023 Men's 'The Hundred' tournament?

49. The Eastenders character of Cindy Beale returned to Albert Square after many years. Who plays her role?

50. Which boxer was controversially defeated in his heavyweight world-title bout by champion Oleksandr Usyk?

August 2023 - Answer

1. Who took a wicket with the final ball of his professional cricket playing career to take the Ashes series to a 2-2 draw? **Stuart Broad**

2. Which member of *The Rolling Stones* celebrated his 80th Birthday? **Mick Jagger**

3. Which team announced that Formula 1 team principal Otmar Szafnauer is leaving them? **Alpine**

4. NASA managed to re establish contact with which spacecraft after a period of silence? Now 12 billion miles away from Earth, it was launched in 1977. **Voyager 2**

5. How many goals in total did England score in their Group D matches at the FIFA Women's World Cup? **Eight**

6. Sadly, Sinead O'Connor passed away in August. What was her first UK Chart Single? **Mandinka**

7. Who was the Host Nation of the Netball World Cup 2023? **South Africa**

8. While Rishi Sunak took a Summer Holiday in California, who was in charge of the country? **Oliver Dowden**

9. Which Olympic diving champion has said he will return to the pool after a two year break to target a spot at Paris 2024? **Tom Daley**

10. Britain's 'Wonkiest Pub' was controversially demolished following a fire. Where was it situated? **Himley near Dudley**

11. Which team put 7 goals past Port Vale in their opening match of the EFL League One Season? **Barnsley**

12. How many people were in the honours list submitted by Liz Truss as an outgoing Prime Minister? **Fourteen**

13. A World Scout Jamboree attracting more than 40,000 from 155 different countries was affected by a tropical storm. In which country was it scheduled? **South Korea**

14. After playing in the Ashes tests, Ben Duckett participated in *The Hundred.* Which team did he play for? **Birmingham Phoenix**

15. Who won the Netball World Cup 2023 tournament? **Australia**

16. Members of Greenpeace staged a protest at the home of Rishi Sunak. In which county is his residence? **North Yorkshire**

17. Filippo Ganna won gold at the World Cycling Championships in the Men's Individual Pursuit. Which country does he represent? **Italy**

18. Who produced one of the most remarkable rounds in the history of golf on Sunday, shooting 58 to win the LIV Golf Greenbrier title? **Bryson DeChambeau**

19. Asylum Seekers were evacuated from the Portland port barge they were housed in after evidence of Legionella bacteria was found in the water supply. What is the name of the barge? **Bibby Stockholm**

20. After scoring against AFC Bournemouth, Mo Salah became Liverpool's 5th highest goal scorer. Can you name the 4 players above him? **Ian Rush 346, Roger Hunt 285, Gordon Hodgson 241 and Billy Liddell 228**

21. What type of aircraft, the only one of its type not to have been fully restored, was flown this month to celebrate its 80th birthday? **A Supermarine Spitfire Mk IX**

22. Which England rugby union player was sent off during their 19-17 defeat of Wales at Twickenham? **Owen Farrell**

23. It was reported that the Duke of Sussex has had their HRH removed on the royal family's website. This coincided with his visit to which country? **Japan**

24. Who became the first woman batter to score a century in *The Hundred* competition? **Tammy Beaumont**

25. Which music magazine's comeback issue sold out within minutes? **NME**

26. Who won their 36th Para-cycling gold at the Cycling World Championships in the C5 individual time trial? **Sarah Storey**

27. An eight foot tall totem pole mysteriously appeared on a nature reserve overlooking the coast of which county? **Kent**

28. The charity Guide Dogs UK suggested that a shortage of guide dogs might be mitigated by using more of which breed? **German Shepherd**

29. Which NFL legend became a minority owner in Birmingham City FC? **Tom Brady**

30. Who won the Women's Football World Cup Final? **Spain**

31. Eight people were rescued from a cable car after one of the cables snapped leaving them stranded 900 feet above a ravine. In which country did this take place? **Pakistan**

32. Le Touquet-Paris-Plage airport announced it was set to be renamed in honour of who? **Queen Elizabeth II**

33. It was reported that the UK's first ever transplant of which organ was carried out at the Churchill Hospital, Oxford last February? **A womb**

34. In MotoGP, Francesco Bagnaia, won the feature race in Austria from pole, extending his world championship lead to 62 points. What is the name of the circuit where this took place? **Red Bull Ring, Spielberg**

35. Why was Lorna Rose Treen in the news this August? **Her joke was voted the funniest of this year's Edinburgh Fringe**

36. Zharnel Hughes won a bronze medal at the World Athletics Championships in the 100m. Which country hosted the event? **Hungary**

37. Several songs from *Barbie the Album* feature on this August's UK Singles Chat. Which artist performed 'Dance The Night'? **Dua Lipa**

38. Harry Brook scored 105 in 42 balls but could not stop his team falling to defeat against Welsh Fire in *The Hundred*. Which team did he play for? **Northern Superchargers**

39. Who was announced to be taking over the presenter's role on the BBC programme *Inside the Factory*? **Paddy McGuiness**

40. In August, Japan began its controversial discharge of treated waste water from which nuclear plant into the Pacific Ocean? **Fukushima**

41. Can you name the 4 Arsenal players named in the PFA Men's Team of the Year? **Aaron Ramsdale, William Saliba, Martin Odergaard and Bukayo Saka**

42. Donald Trump became the first ever former US President to have a 'mugshot' taken. In which US State did this take place? **Georgia**

43. Who won the Silver medal in the Women's Pole Vault at the World Athletics Championships? **No one! Katie Moon and Nina Kennedy decided to share their pole vault gold medal**

44. Which country became the first to successfully land a spacecraft near the South Pole of The Moon? **India**

45. Over one hundred volunteers took part in a search for the *Loch Ness Monster*. Loch Ness is the biggest loch in Scotland by volume, but second in surface area to which other? **Loch Lomond**

46. Which Rugby Union International side beat England for the first time ever at the end of August? **Fiji**

47. Which Rap star asked aspiring Republican presidential candidate Vivek Ramaswamy to stop using his songs? **Eminem**

48. Who won the 2023 Men's 'The Hundred' tournament? **Oval Invincibles**

49. The Eastenders character of Cindy Beale returned to Albert Square after many years. Who plays her role? **Michelle Collins**

50. Which boxer was controversially defeated in his heavyweight world-title bout by champion Oleksandr Usyk? **Daniel Dubois**

September 2023 - Questions

1. B&M stores reportedly stepped in to buy up to 51 Wilko stores. Named after their founders, what were B&M initially called?
2. Amidst the school closures due to RAAC concrete issues, who is the Education Secretary?
3. Which England city's council declared itself 'Effectively Bankrupt'?
4. Which 23 year old golfer won the European Masters to clinch a spot the day after on the European Ryder Cup team as one of the wildcard choices?
5. England and New Zealand completed their International T20 series of 4 matches at Trent Bridge. What were the three prior venues?
6. Yang Guang and Tian Tian are Giant Pandas reportedly returning to China after living in which British zoo since 2011?
7. Which boxer beat Liam Smith by TKO in round 10 of their middleweight rematch in Manchester?
8. Ant and Dec collected the best presenter award at the National Television Awards. How many consecutive years have they won it now? A: 12, B:17, C: 22 or D: 28
9. Hosts France participated in the opening match of the 2023 Rugby World Cup. Who were their Group A opponents?
10. Which member of Steps went straight into number 2 on the UK Album Chart with their solo title *Euphoria*?
11. Which British club was drawn in the same UEFA Champions League group as PSG, AC Milan and Dortmund?
12. At the latest G20 Summit meeting in Delhi, India handed over the presidency to which country?

13. Who won their first grand slam tennis title at The US Open Women's Singles?
14. Who won this year's BBC Celebrity Masterchef?
15. Who scored all of England's points in their opening game of the Rugby World Cup as they beat Argentina 27-10?
16. Who won this year's Mercury Music Prize?
17. Sir Mo Farah ran the final race of his career in a half-marathon at which annual event?
18. Sadly, impressionist Mike Yarwood passed away, aged 82. What line did he deliver before singing a closing song at the end of his TV shows?
19. Which cricket team were deducted three points in the County Championship for preparing a "below average" pitch for their match against Essex in July?
20. The first lot of Sotheby's evening auction: Freddie Mercury, A World of His Own was the Garden Lodge Door. With an estimate of £15,000 to £25,000 it eventually sold for A: £52,750, B: £195,800, C: £304,250 or D: £412,750?
21. Apple has confirmed its new iPhone will not feature its proprietary lightning charging port. Which version of iPhone would this be?
22. In NFL, who defeated Super Bowl holders Kansas City Chiefs in their season opener?
23. Who broke the record score for an England player in a One Day International when they made a sensational 182 runs versus New Zealand at The Oval?
24. Which UK nation became the first to drop their speed limit to 20mph?
25. Who beat Australia after narrowly losing to Wales the previous week at the Rugby World Cup?

26. Which singer who performed songs including 'Durham Town', 'I Don't Believe in it Anymore' and 'The Last Farewell' sadly passed away?
27. Neil Warnock left Huddersfield Town having extended the record he holds for most games managed in professional league football in England to A: 989 B:1,258 C:1,427 or D:1,628?
28. Which long running but interrupted soap opera returned this month on Amazon's Freevee channel?
29. The largest lake in the UK is reported to be significantly poisoned by toxic blue-green algae. What is the name of this lake?
30. Chelsea Pitman, part of England's gold-medal-winning squad at the 2018 Commonwealth Games, announced her retirement at international level from which sport?
31. Prince William revealed a shortlist of 15 contenders for this year's Earthshot Prize in which US city?
32. The Solheim Cup is a tournament in what sport?
33. A pair of used theatre tickets for Ford Theatre fetched a reported £215,423 at a Boston, Massachusetts auction. What was so special about them?
34. At which NFL stadium was Taylor Swift widely pictured this month? (Team or Stadium Name)?
35. NASA successfully landed a sample taken from an asteroid for the first time. What was the asteroid called?
36. Tigist Assefa broke the Women's marathon record in Berlin. Which country does she represent?
37. Newcastle United set a Premier League record when eight different players scored in the game with Sheffield United. How many can you name?
38. Which seaside town was the venue for this year's Lib Dem conference?

39. *Hackney Diamonds* is the new album from which legendary band?

40. It was reported that the development of the UK's largest untapped oil field had been approved by regulators. What is it called?

September 2023 - Answers

1. B&M stores reportedly stepped in to buy up to 51 Wilko stores. Named after their founders, what were B&M initially called? **Billington and Mayman**

2. Amidst the school closures due to RAAC concrete issues, who is the Education Secretary? **Gillian Keegan**

3. Which England city's council declared itself 'Effectively Bankrupt'? **Birmingham**

4. Which 23 year old golfer won the European Masters on Sunday to clinch a spot the day after on the European Ryder Cup team as one of the wildcard choices? **Ludvig Aberg**

5. England and New Zealand completed their International T20 series of 4 matches at Trent Bridge. What were the three prior venues? **Durham, Old Trafford and Edgbaston**

6. Yang Guang and Tian Tian are Giant Pandas reportedly returning to China after living in which British zoo since 2011? **Edinburgh**

7. Which boxer beat Liam Smith by TKO in round 10 of their middleweight rematch in Manchester? **Chris Eubank Jr.**

8. Ant and Dec collected the best presenter award at the National Television Awards. How many consecutive years have they won it now? A: 12, B:17, C: 22 or D: 28 **C**

9. Hosts France participated in the opening match of the 2023 Rugby World Cup. Who were their Group A opponents? **New Zealand**

10. Which member of Steps went straight into number 2 on the UK Album Chart with their solo title *Euphoria*? **Claire Richards**

11. Which British club was drawn in the same UEFA Champions League group as PSG, AC Milan and Dortmund? **Newcastle United**

12. At the latest G20 Summit meeting in Delhi, India handed over the presidency to which country? **Brazil**

13. Who won their first grand slam tennis title at The US Open Women's Singles? **Coco Gauff**

14. Who won this year's BBC Celebrity Masterchef? **Wynne Evans**

15. Who scored all of England's points in their opening game of the Rugby World Cup as they beat Argentina 27-10? **George Ford**

16. Who won this year's Mercury Music Prize? **Ezra Collective**

17. Sir Mo Farah ran the final race of his career in a half-marathon at which annual event? **The Great North Run**

18. Sadly, impressionist Mike Yarwood passed away, aged 82. What line did he deliver before singing a closing song at the end of his TV shows? **And This Is Me**

19. Which cricket team were deducted three points in the County Championship for preparing a "below average" pitch for their match against Essex in July? **Hampshire**

20. The first lot of Sotheby's evening auction: Freddie Mercury, A World of His Own was the Garden Lodge Door. With an estimate of £15,000 to £25,000 it eventually sold for A: £52,750, B: £195,800, C: £304,250 or D: £412,750? **D**

21. Apple has confirmed its new iPhone will not feature its proprietary lightning charging port. Which version of iPhone will this be? **iPhone15**

22. In NFL, who defeated Super Bowl holders Kansas City Chiefs in their season opener? **Detroit Lions**

23. Who broke the record score for an England player in a One Day International when they made a sensational 182 runs versus New Zealand at The Oval? **Ben Stokes**

24. Which UK nation became the first to drop their speed limit to 20mph? **Wales**

25. Who beat Australia after narrowly losing to Wales the previous week at the Rugby World Cup? **Fiji**

26. Which singer who performed songs including 'Durham Town', 'I Don't Believe in it Anymore' and 'The Last Farewell' sadly passed away? **Roger Whittaker**

27. Neil Warnock left Huddersfield Town having extended the record he holds for most games managed in professional league football in England to A: 989 B:1,258 C:1,427 or D:1,628? **D**

28. Which long running but interrupted soap opera returned this month on Amazon's Freevee channel? **Neighbours**

29. The largest lake in the UK is reported to be significantly poisoned by toxic blue-green algae. What is the name of this lake? **Lough Neagh**

30. Chelsea Pitman, part of England's gold-medal-winning squad at the 2018 Commonwealth Games, announced her retirement at international level from which sport? **Netball**

31. Prince William revealed a shortlist of 15 contenders for this year's Earthshot Prize in which US city? **New York**

32. The Solheim Cup is a tournament in what sport? **Golf**

33. A pair of used theatre tickets for Ford Theatre fetched a reported £215,423 at a Boston, Massachusetts auction. What was so special about them? **They were used at the performance where President Abraham Lincoln was assassinated.**

34. At which NFL stadium was Taylor Swift widely pictured? (Team or Stadium Name)? **Kansas City Chiefs, Arrowhead Stadium**

35. NASA successfully landed a sample taken from an asteroid for the first time. What was the asteroid called? **Bennu**

36. Tigist Assefa broke the Women's marathon record in Berlin. Which country does she represent? **Ethiopia**

37. Newcastle United set a Premier League record when eight different players scored in the game with Sheffield United. How many can you name? **Longstaff, Burn, Botman, Wilson, Gordon, Almirón, Guimães and Isak**

38. Which seaside town was the venue for this year's Lib Dem conference? **Bournemouth**

39. *Hackney Diamonds* is the new album from which legendary band? **The Rolling Stones**

40. It was reported that the development of the UK's largest untapped oil field has been approved by regulators. What is it called? **Rosebank**

October 2023 - Questions

1. The felling of the tree in the Hadrian's Wall gap caused a major outcry. What type of tree was it?
2. Europe won the Ryder Cup. In which country was the tournament held?
3. In cricket, which team retained the County Championship title?
4. In which city was the Conservative Party conference held?
5. Who scored a hat-trick as Aston Villa thrashed Brighton and Hove Albion 6-1?
6. Who became the first celebrity to leave Strictly Come Dancing?
7. At the Rugby World Cup, how many points did Scotland score against Romania without reply?
8. Astronaut Frank Rubio returned to Earth after spending a record amount of time on a space flight. How many days was he in space for? A: 98 days, B: 179 days, C: 295 days or D: 371 days
9. Which team were beaten by Jacksonville Jaguars in the first match of the NFL International Series at Wembley?
10. Which new Las Vegas venue opened with a residency by U2?
11. Where in Belgium were the World Gymnastics Championships held?
12. Which famous actor who sadly passed away this month, had a corner on the Top Gear track named after him?
13. South Africa hit a record Cricket World Cup total against Sri Lanka. Was their 50 overs score: A: 328, B: 378, C: 428 or D: 478?

14. Which political party won the Rutherglen and Hamilton West by-election?

15. Who became the first female football referee to oversee a men's international at Wembley Stadium when England played against Australia?

16. Who co-hosted the new ITV based Big Brother with Will Best?

17. Which UK airport had to suspend flights after a fire in one of the car parks?

18. A set of all 4 autographs by The Beatles collected at their MBE ceremony was sold at auction this month for how much? A: £740, B: £7,400, C: £74,000 or D: £740,000

19. In spite of having a restriction on the number of laps that could be done on their tyres in the F1 Qatar Grand Prix, which company had their contract extended until 2027?

20. What creature was the subject of the photo that won Wildlife Photographer of the Year for Laurent Ballesta, an award he has now won twice?

21. Ed Sheeran had a new album at the top of the UK Charts. What is it called?

22. Which couple became the first to receive a 10 in the latest series of Strictly Come Dancing?

23. Who recorded their first ever Rugby World Cup win when they beat Fiji by 24-23?

24. Daniel Noboa was set to become the youngest president of which South American country after winning October's run off election?

25. By what margin did South Africa beat France in the Rugby World Cup Quarter Final?

26. Which fashion chain reportedly showed an interest in buying the Fat Face brand, having already bought rivals such as Cath Kidson and JoJo Maman Bebé?

27. Who beat England's cricketers to inflict their second defeat in the World Cup ODI tournament and record only their second win in the competition's history?

28. Who was the first evictee from the Big Brother house?

29. It was reported that the sliding events of the 2026 Winter Olympics will be held outside which host nation after a decision not to invest in a new or refurbished track?

30. Japan Airlines reportedly scheduled an extra flight to accommodate passengers after concerns about weight limits being exceeded by a number of participants travelling to what type of event?

31. Which TV programme celebrated its 65th anniversary this week?

32. Rory McIlroy and Anthony Joshua are 2 of the sports stars reported to have invested in which F1 team?

33. Who was reportedly the subject of a 9 million pound settlement following his serious crash while presenting Top Gear?

34. Which Rugby League team mounted a stunning fightback to win at Toulouse Olympique in the Championship Grand Final to gain promotion back to the Super League?

35. The Joint European Torus project is coming to an end after 40 years of testing. What process has it been used to investigate?

36. By what margin did South Africa beat England in the Rugby World Cup Semi-Final?

37. With *Movember* fast approaching, we were reminded that the fund-raising initiative is now, how many years old? A: 10, B: 15, C: 20 or D: 25

38. Who was disqualified after finishing second at the Austin, Texas F1 Grand Prix?

39. *Are We There Yet?* is the title of a new album released by which artist?

40. Which South African cricketer hit 174 runs in their ODI World Cup match against Bangladesh?

41. Which constituency in Staffordshire saw a huge Tory majority overturned by Labour in a by election?

42. Sadly, legendary footballer Sir Bobby Charlton passed away in October. How many caps did he have for a England for whom he scored 49 goals? A: 91, B: 96, C: 101, D: 106

43. Which well known book is celebrated by this year's release of a Christmas 50p piece by The Royal Mint, the first Christmas issue to feature King Charles on the reverse?

44. Players of which sport started a new season competing for the Larry O'Brien Championship Trophy?

45. By what margin did South Africa beat New Zealand in the Rugby World Cup Final?

October 2023 - Answers

1. Europe won the Ryder Cup. In which country was the tournament held? **Italy**
2. The felling of the tree in the Hadrian's Wall gap caused a major outcry. What type of tree was it? **Sycamore**
3. In cricket, which team retained the County Championship title? **Surrey**
4. In which city was the Conservative Party conference held? **Manchester**
5. Who scored a hat-trick as Aston Villa thrashed Brighton and Hove Albion 6-1? **Ollie Watkins**
6. Who became the first celebrity to leave Strictly Come Dancing? **Les Dennis**
7. At the Rugby World Cup, how many points did Scotland score against Romania without reply? **84**
8. Astronaut Frank Rubio returned to Earth after spending a record amount of time on a space flight. How many days was he in space for? A: 98 days, B: 179 days, C: 295 days or D: 371 days. **D**
9. Which team were beaten by Jacksonville Jaguars in the first match of the NFL International Series at Wembley? **Atlanta Falcons**
10. Which new Las Vegas venue opened with a residency by U2? **The Sphere**
11. Where in Belgium were the World Gymnastics Championships held? **Antwerp**
12. Which famous actor who sadly passed away this month, had a corner on the Top Gear track named after him? **Sir Michael Gambon**

13. South Africa hit a record Cricket World Cup total against Sri Lanka. Was their 50 overs score: A: 328, B: 378, C: 428 or D: 478? **C**

14. Which political party won the Rutherglen and Hamilton West by-election? **Scottish Labour Party**

15. Who became the first female football referee to oversee a men's international at Wembley Stadium when England played against Australia? **Stephanie Frappart**

16. Who co-hosted the new ITV based Big Brother with Will Best? **AJ Odudu**

17. Which UK airport had to suspend flights after a fire in one of the car parks? **Luton Airport**

18. A set of all 4 autographs by The Beatles collected at their MBE ceremony was sold at auction this month for how much? A: £740, B: £7,400, C: £74,000 or D: £740,000 **B**

19. In spite of having a restriction on the number of laps that could be done on their tyres in the F1 Qatar Grand Prix, which company had their contract extended until 2027? **Pirelli**

20. What creature was the subject of the photo that won Wildlife Photographer of the Year for Laurent Ballesta, an award he has now won twice? **A horseshoe crab**

21. Ed Sheeran had a new album at the top of the UK Charts. What is it called? **Autumn Variations**

22. Which couple became the first to receive a 10 in the latest series of Strictly Come Dancing? **Eddie Kadi and Karen Hauer**

23. Who recorded their first ever Rugby World Cup win when they beat Fiji by 24-23? **Portugal**

24. Daniel Noboa was set to become the youngest president of which South American country after winning October's run off election? **Ecuador**

25. By what margin did South Africa beat France in the Rugby World Cup Quarter Final? **One Point**

26. Which fashion chain reportedly showed an interest in buying the Fat Face brand, having already bought rivals such as Cath Kidson and JoJo Maman Bebé? **Next**

27. Who beat England's cricketers to inflict their second defeat in the World Cup ODI tournament and record only their second win in the competition's history? **Afghanistan**

28. Who was the first evictee from the Big Brother house? **Farida Khalifa**

29. It was reported that the sliding events of the 2026 Winter Olympics will be held outside which host nation after a decision not to invest in a new or refurbished track? **Italy**

30. Japan Airlines reportedly scheduled an extra flight to accommodate passengers after concerns about weight limits being exceeded by a number of participants travelling to what type of event? **A Sumo Wrestling competition**

31. Which TV programme celebrated its 65th anniversary this week? **Blue Peter**

32. Rory McIlroy and Anthony Joshua are 2 of the sports stars reported to have invested in which F1 team? **Alpine**

33. Who was reportedly the subject of a 9 million pound settlement following his serious crash while presenting Top Gear? **Andrew Flintoff**

34. Which Rugby League team mounted a stunning fightback to win at Toulouse Olympique in the Championship Grand Final to gain promotion back to the Super League? **London Broncos**

35. The Joint European Torus project is coming to an end after 40 years of testing. What process has it been used to investigate? **Nuclear Fusion**

36. By what margin did South Africa beat England in the Rugby World Cup Semi-Final? **One Point**

37. With *Movember* fast approaching, we were reminded that the fund-raising initiative is now, how many years old? A:10, B: 15, C: 20 or D: 25 **C**

38. Who was disqualified after finishing second at the Austin, Texas F1 Grand Prix? **Lewis Hamilton**

39. *Are We There Yet?* is the title of a new album released by which artist? **Rick Astley**

40. Which South African cricketer hit 174 runs in their ODI World Cup match against Bangladesh? **Quinton de Kock**

41. Which constituency in Staffordshire saw a huge Tory majority overturned by Labour in a by election? **Tamworth**

42. Sadly, legendary footballer Sir Bobby Charlton passed away in October. How many caps did he have for a England for whom he scored 49 goals? A: 91, B: 96, C: 101, D: 106 **D:106**

43. Which well known book is celebrated by this year's release of a Christmas 50p piece by The Royal Mint, the first Christmas issue to feature King Charles on the reverse? **The Snowman**

44. Players of which sport started a new season competing for the Larry O'Brien Championship Trophy? **NBA Basketball**

45. By what margin did South Africa beat New Zealand in the Rugby World Cup Final? **One Point**

November 2023 - Questions

1. In the first week of November, Taylor Swift had no fewer than five albums in the UK Top 20 album chart. How many can you name?
2. Who captained England's team at the ODI Cricket World Cup?
3. Who did England's Rugby League team defeat in each of their three tests?
4. It was reported that plans to close rail ticket offices in England had been scrapped. Who was the current Transport Secretary?
5. It was announced that, starting in the New Year, Boris Johnson will host a show on which TV Station?
6. Which African country hosted a state visit by King Charles?
7. Which country decided against making a bid to host the FIFA World Cup in 2034, leaving Saudi Arabia as the only bidder?
8. Who resigned their post as Head Coach of Australia's Rugby Union team after barely 9 months in the role?
9. Which two letter word was given the title of "word of the year" by the makers of Collins Dictionary?
10. Who lost on a split decision to Tyson Fury on his professional boxing debut in Riyadh?
11. In which country did Prince William announce the winners of the 2023 Earthshot Prize?
12. Which National League side won 7-4 away to Swindon Town in the FA Cup first round?
13. What was the name given to the storm that caused significant damage in the Channel Islands?

14. In what way was Angelo Mathews controversially dismissed during Sri Lanka's match against Bangladesh in the ODI World Cup?

15. Barbra Streisand released her memoirs. What is the name of her book?

16. Which driver crashed out of the F1 Grand Prix at Interlagos during the formation lap?

17. Orchestral Manoeuvres in the Dark released a new album that entered the charts at No. 2. What is it called?

18. Ethiopian Tamirat Tola broke a 12-year-old course record as he won a men's marathon race in November. In which city was this held?

19. It was reported that an original 19th century photograph of a thatcher had been found. Most likely Lot Long from Mere in Wiltshire. On which iconic album cover of the 1970's did it feature?

20. An image of the Horsehead Nebula was among the first to be released from which European Space Telescope?

21. Denis O'Regan became the first jump jockey to ride a winner at every British and Irish National Hunt racecourse. At which venue did he finally achieve a win to complete this feat?

22. A statue of Lemmy from Motörhead was proposed in his birthplace. In which of the Five Towns of Stoke-on-Trent was he born?

23. Where did England's Men's cricket team finish in the ICC ODI World Cup Table?

24. Who became the new UK Government Home Secretary after the departure of Suella Braverman?

25. In which sport did Great Britain qualify for next year's finals of the BJK Cup?

26. Which country declared a state of emergency after a series of earthquakes raised fears of a volcanic eruption?

27. Who won the women's individual trampoline gold at the Trampolining and Tumbling World Championships held in Birmingham?

28. Chelsea boss Emma Hayes has been named the new manager of which country's women's national team who she will join next year?

29. Back to Taylor Swift, who added an additional two nights at Wembley Stadium after the existing shows on her tour there sold out. What is the title of her tour?

30. In which sport did Enea Bastianini claim his first win of the season in Malaysia?

31. King Charles III celebrated his birthday. What age is he now?

32. Who became the new ODI Cricket World Cup Champions after beating the hosts in the final?

33. Who is the director of the newly released movie about Napoleon?

34. How many points were Everton FC deducted by the Premier League, putting them 19th in the table?

35. Who is the new president of Argentina?

36. Which couple left Strictly Come Dancing directly after the show in Blackpool?

37. Vernon Kay completed his Children In Need Ultramarathon arriving in Bolton. From which city did he begin this challenge?

38. In which Scottish city were the European Curling Championships held?

39. The Cambridge Dictionary's Word of the Year is also the title of a song performed by Dua Lipa. What is it?

40. President Biden held a meeting with the Chinese President. What is his name?

41. Which former Wales Rugby Union Captain played the final game of his career when he turned out for Toulon?
42. Which hit Netflix hit returned to our screens, but this time in the form of a reality game show?
43. According to reports, which OpenAI co-founder was set to return as boss just days after he was fired by the board?
44. What annual award was won by Paul Lynch?
45. Which country won their first Davis Cup title in 47 years?
46. Which country's government reportedly plans to scrap the nation's world-leading smoking ban to fund tax cuts?
47. Sadly, Terry Venables passed away aged 80. As well as managing England, which Spanish club did he manage in the mid-nineteen eighties?
48. How many of the F1 season's 23 races were won by Max Verstappen?
49. Which of Jupiter's moons is the planned destination of a NASA spacecraft that will carry the names of people who subscribe to have their name stencilled onto a microchip?
50. Which former winners of the FA Cup were thrown out of the tournament after fielding an ineligible player in their First Round replay?
51. Which institution became the subject of a new book 'Endgame' by Omid Scobie?
52. Who won his third major darts tournament in two months after beating Michael Van Gerwen at the PDC Players Championship Finals in Minehead?
53. The campmates in 'I'm a Celebrity Get Me Out of Here' were joined by a couple of late arrivals from the sports world. Who were they?

November 2023 - Answers

1. In the first week of November, Taylor Swift had no fewer than five albums in the UK Top 20 album chart. How many can you name? **Lover, Reputation, Folklore, 1989 and Midnights**

2. Who captained England's team at the ODI Cricket World Cup? **Joss Buttler**

3. Who did England's Rugby League team defeat in each of their three tests? **Tonga**

4. It was reported that plans to close rail ticket offices in England had been scrapped. Who was the current Transport Secretary? **Mark Harper**

5. It was announced that, starting in the New Year, Boris Johnson will host a show on which TV Station? **GB News**

6. Which African country hosted a state visit by King Charles? **Kenya**

7. Which country decided against making a bid to host the FIFA World Cup in 2034, leaving Saudi Arabia as the only bidder? **Australia**

8. Who resigned their post as Head Coach of Australia's Rugby Union team after barely 9 months in the role? **Eddie Jones**

9. Which two letter word was given the title of "word of the year" by the makers of Collins Dictionary? **AI**

10. Who lost on a split decision to Tyson Fury on his professional boxing debut in Riyadh? **Francis Ngannou**

11. In which country did Prince William announce the winners of the 2023 Earthshot Prize? **Singapore**

12. Which National League side won 7-4 away to Swindon Town in the FA Cup first round? **Aldershot**

13. What was the name given to the storm that caused significant damage in the Channel Islands? **Storm Ciarán**

14. In what way was Angelo Mathews controversially dismissed during Sri Lanka's match against Bangladesh in the ODI World Cup? **Timed Out**

15. Barbra Streisand released her memoirs. What is the name of her book? **My Name is Barbra**

16. Which driver crashed out of the F1 Grand Prix at Interlagos during the formation lap? **Charles LeClerc**

17. Orchestral Manoeuvres in the Dark released a new album that entered the charts at No. 2. What is it called? **Bauhaus Staircase**

18. Ethiopian Tamirat Tola broke a 12-year-old course record as he won a men's marathon race in November. In which city was this held? **New York City**

19. It was reported that an original 19th century photograph of a thatcher had been found. Most likely Lot Long from Mere in Wiltshire. On which iconic album cover of the 1970's did it feature? **Led Zeppelin IV**

20. An image of the Horsehead Nebula was among the first to be released from which European Space Telescope? **Euclid**

21. Denis O'Regan became the first jump jockey to ride a winner at every British and Irish National Hunt racecourse. At which venue did he finally achieve a win to complete this feat? **Hereford**

22. A statue of Lemmy from Motörhead was proposed in his birthplace. In which of the Five Towns of Stoke-on-Trent was he born? **Burslem**

23. Where did England's Men's cricket team finish in the ICC ODI World Cup Table? **7th**

24. Who became the new UK Government Home Secretary after the departure of Suella Braverman? **James Cleverly**

25. In which sport did Great Britain qualify for next year's finals of the BJK Cup? **Tennis**

26. Which country declared a state of emergency after a series of earthquakes raised fears of a volcanic eruption? **Iceland**

27. Who won the women's individual trampoline gold at the Trampolining and Tumbling World Championships held in Birmingham? **Bryony Page**

28. Chelsea boss Emma Hayes has been named the new manager of which country's women's national team who she will join next year? **USA**

29. Back to Taylor Swift, who added an additional two nights at Wembley Stadium after the existing shows on her tour there sold out. What is the title of her tour? **ERAS**

30. In which sport did Enea Bastianini claim his first win of the season in Malaysia? **Moto GP (motorcycling)**

31. King Charles III celebrated his birthday. What age is he now? **75**

32. Who became the new ODI Cricket World Cup Champions after beating the hosts in the final? **Australia**

33. Who is the director of the newly released movie about Napoleon? **Ridley Scott**

34. How many points were Everton FC deducted by the Premier League, putting them 19th in the table? **10**

35. Who is the new president of Argentina? **Javier Milei**

36. Which couple left Strictly Come Dancing directly after the show in Blackpool? **Angela (Rippon) and Kai**

37. Vernon Kay completed his Children In Need Ultramarathon arriving in Bolton. From which city did he begin this challenge? **Leicester**

38. In which Scottish city were the European Curling Championships held? **Aberdeen**

39. The Cambridge Dictionary's Word of the Year is also the title of a song performed by Dua Lipa. What is it? **Hallucinate**

40. President Biden held a meeting with the Chinese President. What is his name? **Xi Jinping**

41. Which former Wales Rugby Union Captain played the final game of his career when he turned out for Toulon? **Alun Wyn Jones**

42. Which hit Netflix hit returned to our screens, but this time in the form of a reality game show? **Squid Game**

43. According to reports, which OpenAI co-founder was set to return as boss just days after he was fired by the board? **Sam Altman**

44. What annual award was won by Paul Lynch? **The Booker Prize**

45. Which country won their first Davis Cup title in 47 years? **Italy**

46. Which country's government reportedly plans to scrap the nation's world-leading smoking ban to fund tax cuts? **New Zealand**

47. Sadly, Terry Venables passed away aged 80. As well as managing England, which Spanish club did he manage in the mid-nineteen eighties? **Barcelona**

48. How many of the F1 season's 23 races were won by Max Verstappen? **19**

49. Which of Jupiter's moons is the planned destination of a NASA spacecraft that will carry the names of people who subscribe to have their name stencilled onto a microchip? **Europa**

50. Which former winners of the FA Cup were thrown out of the tournament after fielding an ineligible player in their First Round replay? **Barnsley**

51. Which institution became the subject of a new book 'Endgame' by Omid Scobie? **The Royal Family**

52. Who won his third major darts tournament in two months after beating Michael Van Gerwen at the PDC Players Championship Finals in Minehead? **Luke Humphries**

53. The campmates in 'I'm a Celebrity Get Me Out of Here' were joined by a couple of late arrivals from the sports world. Who were they? **Frankie Dettori and Tony Bellew**

December 2023 - Questions

1. Which Bar in Enniskillen, County Fermanagh, posted a Christmas advert style video that quickly went viral racking up millions of views on social media?

2. What is the location of the 2023 BBC Sports Personality of the Year?

3. Netflix continued releasing more Episodes of The Crown, what number series has it reached?

4. Which three home nations featured in the draw for the UEFA Euro 24 Finals in Germany?

5. Christmas Jumper Day is organised by which charity?

6. Where in London could you visit Glide, an ice rink which also boasts a 30 foot Christmas Tree?

7. Where was the Cop28 climate summit held until December 12? **UAE**

8. Birmingham has now hosted a German Christmas market since 2001. With which German city is it associated?

9. Reports emerged in September that Eastenders Actors had been requested not to appear in Pantomime next year. This is said to be so they are available for filming the soap's 40th anniversary. Eastenders is 40 years old in 2025. Nevertheless, there are plenty appearing all over the land in 2023. Can you name the actors or their Eastenders characters playing the following roles?

    A: Prince Frederick, Snow White and the Seven Dwarfs, Aylesbury.

    B: Buttons, Cinderella, Milton Keynes

    C: Flesh Creep, Jack and the Beanstalk, Dunstable

    D: Belle, Beauty and the Beast, Dartford

E: Abanazaar, Aladdin, Chatham

F: Dick Whittington, Dick Whittington, Nottingham

10. In the Netherlands, seasonal celebrations get underway with Sinterklaas Eve on December 5th. Sinterklaas travels on a creature named Amerigo. Is Amerigo A: A Camel, B: A Reindeer, C: A Donkey or D: A Horse?

11. David Tennant and Catherine Tate returned to Dr Who in a series of special episodes that marked which anniversary of the programme?

12. The Royal Mail has issued 5 stamps for Christmas 2023. On each is a line from a Christmas Carol. Can you name the five carols? (To make it easier, the lines from each stamp are as follows:)

   A. 2nd Class Stamp "O hear the angel voices"

   B. 1st Class Stamp "All is calm, all is bright"

   C. 2nd Class Large Stamp "The silent stars go by"

   D. 1st Class Stamp "Asleep on the hay"

   E. £2.20 Stamp "Star of wonder, star of night"

13. In a move, criticised by some supporters, which Premier League football match was rescheduled to Christmas Eve 2023, the first EPL match to be so since 1995?

14. Who are the six celebrities taking part in this years Strictly Come Dancing Christmas Special?

15. Actors Matthew Baynton and Simon Farnaby from Horrible Histories both appear in which December movie release?

16. Observation of the celebration of Kwanzaa runs from 26 December to 1st January. In which year was it created? A:1966, B:1976, C:1986, D:1996

17. Who is set to take over BBC Radio 2 Saturday Morning's show from Claudia Winkelman in the New Year?

18. Which Railway Union's members voted to accept a pay offer from rail operating companies?

19. Which two cities saw the first reopening of *Wilko* stores at the beginning of the month?

20. The Automobile Association has advised drivers to avoid what as they may potentially conceal potholes?

December 2023 - Answers

1. Which Bar in Enniskillen, County Fermanagh, posted a Christmas advert style video that quickly went viral racking up millions of views on social media? **Charlie's Bar**

2. What is the location of the 2023 BBC Sports Personality of the Year? **Media City, Salford**

3. Netflix continued releasing more Episodes of The Crown, what number series has it reached? **Six**

4. Which three home nations featured in the draw for the UEFA Euro 24 Finals in Germany? **England, Scotland and Wales**

5. Christmas Jumper Day is organised by which charity? **Save the Children**

6. Where in London could you visit Glide, an ice rink which also boasts a 30 foot Christmas Tree? **Battersea Power Station**

7. Where was the Cop28 climate summit held until December 12? **UAE, Dubai**

8. Birmingham has now hosted a German Christmas market since 2001. With which German city is it associated? **Frankfurt**

9. Reports emerged in September that Eastenders Actors had been requested not to appear in Pantomime next year. This is said to be so they are available for filming the soap's 40th anniversary. Eastenders is 40 years old in 2025. Nevertheless, there are plenty appearing all over the land in 2023. Can you name the actors or their Eastenders characters playing the following roles?

A: Prince Frederick, Snow White and the Seven Dwarfs, Aylesbury. **James Bye/Martin Fowler**

B: Buttons, Cinderella, Milton Keynes **Brian Conley/Rocky Cotton**

C: Flesh Creep, Jack and the Beanstalk, Dunstable **Steve McFadden/Phil Mitchell**

D: Belle, Beauty and the Beast, Dartford **Shona McGarty/Whitney Dean**

E: Abanazaar, Aladdin, Chatham **Delroy Atkinson/ Howie Danes**

F: Dick Whittington, Dick Whittington, Nottingham **Shane Richie/Alfie Moon**

10. In the Netherlands, seasonal celebrations get underway with Sinterklaas Eve on December 5th. Sinterklaas travels on a creature named Amerigo. Is Amerigo A: A Camel, B: A Reindeer, C: A Donkey or D: A Horse? **D: A Horse**

11. David Tennant and Catherine Tate returned to Dr Who in a series of special episodes that marked which anniversary of the programme? **60 years**

12. The Royal Mail has issued 5 stamps for Christmas 2023. On each is a line from a Christmas Carol. Can you name the five carols? (To make it easier, the lines from each stamp are as follows:)

    A. 2nd Class Stamp "O hear the angel voices" **O Holy Night**

    B. 1st Class Stamp "All is calm, all is bright" **Silent Night**

    C. 2nd Class Large Stamp "The silent stars go by" **O Little Town of Bethlehem**

    D. 1st Class Stamp "Asleep on the hay" **Away in a Manger**

E. £2.20 Stamp "Star of wonder, star of night" **We three kings**

13. In a move, criticised by some supporters, which Premier League football match was rescheduled to Christmas Eve 2023, the first EPL match to be so since 1995? **Wolverhampton Wanderers v Chelsea**

14. Who are the six celebrities taking part in this years Strictly Come Dancing Christmas Special? **Danny Cipriani, Keisha Buchanan, Tillie Amartey, Dan Snow, Jamie Borthwick and Sally Nugent**

15. Actors Matthew Baynton and Simon Farnaby from Horrible Histories both appear in which December movie release? **Wonka**

16. Observation of the celebration of Kwanzaa runs from 26 December to 1st January. In which year was it created? A:1966, B:1976, C:1986, D:1996 **A:1966**

17. Who is set to take over BBC Radio 2 Saturday Morning's show from Claudia Winkelman in the New Year? **Romesh Ranganathan**

18. Which Railway Union's members voted to accept a pay offer from rail operating companies? **RMT**

19. Which two cities saw the first reopening of *Wilko* stores at the beginning of the month? **Exeter and Plymouth**

20. The Automobile Association has advised drivers to avoid what as they may potentially conceal potholes? **Puddles**

Books By This Author

From Rotherham to Rotterdam – An Aston Villa Quiz Book

This book newly published in November 2023 is a real treat for all senior Villa fans. Rekindle memories of the journey from 3rd Division also rans (1971) to Champions of Europe (1982) by answering the 500 questions and teasers that celebrate football from an era happily free from The Premier League and VAR

Ask Me Another, The Ultimate Quiz Book for all things World Cup

Written just before the latest tournament in Qatar 2022. Plenty to test the knowledge of any football supporter right back to the first World Cup in 1930.

Ask Me Another, The BIG QUIZ of 2022

Just like this book but with 450 questions on the Year 2022!

Thank You

Thank you for choosing this book. I think you may be surprised about how important reviews are in helping the independent publisher gain traction among the thousands upon thousands of books on sale.

If you can find the small amount of time it takes to leave a review:

It would be very much appreciated.

Printed in Great Britain
by Amazon